THE END-TIME DAUGHTERS OF THE KING

(Arise And Shine! For The Time Is Short!)

By Monica M. Tomtania

Copyright © 2008 by Monica M. Tomtania

The End-Time Daughters of The King
(Arise And Shine! For The Time Is Short!)
by Monica M. Tomtania

Printed in the United States of America

ISBN 978-1-60477-387-3

All rights reserved solely by the author. The author guarantees all contents are original and do not infringe upon the legal rights of any other person or work. No part of this book may be reproduced in any form without the permission of the author. The views expressed in this book are not necessarily those of the publisher.

Unless otherwise indicated, Bible quotations are taken from the King James Version of THE HOLY BIBLE, Copyright © 1980 by World Bible Society, and the New International Version of THE HOLY BIBLE, Copyright © 1973, 1978, 1984 by International Bible Society.

Registration No TXu1-228-887 (Library of Congress)

www.xulonpress.com

THE END-TIME DAUGHTERS OF THE KING

BY MONICA M. TOMTANIA

DEDICATION

This book is dedicated to all the End-Time Daughters of The King of kings, who are rising up to fulfill their callings, and to grace their destiny with the glory of God—in bringing many sons and daughters into the Kingdom. To God be all the glory through Christ Jesus our Lord, and our soon coming King! "Even so, come, Lord." MARANATHA!

HEARING THE FATHER'S HEART MINISTRIES INT.
7010 MULBERRY COURT
DUBLIN, CA 94568
monicatomtania@yahoo.com

TABLE OF CONTENTS

- *Acknowledgement* .... *xi*
- *Recommendation* .... *xii*
- *Foreword* .... *xix*
1. The Spirit's Cry 25
2. The Prophecy 33
3. The Beginning 39
4. Let's Tell Her Story 61
5. The Problem 83
6. End-Time Vessels 101
7. Women Who Have Been Through The Fire 105
8. Women Who Have Been Through The Waters 125
9. Women Who Have Entered Into
    The King's Chamber 153
10. Access Into The Inner Chamber 173
11. Women Who Have Stripped Off Self 209
12. Women Who Live Under Authority 223
13. Women Who Have Armed Themselves
    For Battle 245
14. Ordinary, Yet Extraordinary 271
15. The Final Words 285
16. Appendixes 295-297

ACKNOWLEDGEMENTS

To My Heavenly Father: Lord, You are really amazing. My knowledge of You is nothing compared to Your Greatness. I give You all the glory!

To my Lord and Savior, Jesus Christ: Thank You very much for saving and choosing me to deliver this message to all Your daughters. I give You all the glory!

Thank You dear Holy Spirit for the inspiration, the insight, and Your enabling power, inspiring me to write, and convey this message in its simplicity to Your people. I give You all the glory!

Special thanks to Don and Faith Magallanes: Your prayers and financial support has made this project a success. Faith, I owe you a big 'Thank you' for helping me with the manuscript.

Mrs. Jan Burkholder, thank you very much for the encouragement and the last touch on the manuscript. You were really great.

Last of all, may God bless all of you from whom I have drawn inspiration and encouragement.

TO GOD BE ALL THE GLORY NOW AND FOREVER MORE!!

RECOMMENDATIONS

"Sister Monica is a woman of God with a burning passion to share the life- changing message of God's Word. ... Without doubt, God has called and anointed this choice servant for such a time as this.'
(Rev. Bob Wilburn - Assistant Supt. Mississippi District and Foreign Missions Director)

* * * * * * *

"Sister Monica is a choice handmaiden of the Lord. Her passion for the Lord, her love and compassion for hurting people, and her understanding of the Word makes her a worthy vessel of the Lord. She has served in different capacities that have brought many blessings to the Churches in this area. She has served as counselor and staff member at the Mississippi Teen Challenge. Sister Tomtania has also held several services in the local churches, and series of teachings for the ladies at Three Rivers Assembly of God. She has also ministered in several of our states."
(Rev. Gene Emswiler, Senior Pastor of Three Rivers Assembly of God, Mississippi & Former Executive Presbyter of the Mississippi District)

* * * * * * *

"As missionaries to Africa for 36 years, we have found Monica to be a woman of God and a minister of integrity. We worked with her and the husband since 1978 and recommend her for ministry ..."
(Rev. Ted Schultz - Missionary to Togo & Benin for 36years - (Hattiesburg, Mississippi)

* * * * * * *

As I read the last word of this manuscript, my mind and spirit were stirred. What can I say? I know that anyone who reads the pages will be blessed as I have been.

It has been a real privilege of mine, as well as that of my family, to know Monica for the last five to six years. She has allowed me to become "Mother" to her third son, Sam. She entrusted this son who is so precious to her "into my keeping" in spite of the fact that she did not really know me. Only God knew what kind of friendship would take place through this trust. Through Sam, the entire Tomtania family has become part of our family, even though we have not met the other boys at this time. I am looking forward to that day.

The love, joy, and peace, that indwells within Monica is so evident and she has instilled that into her boys. Her faith has been such a blessing to all she comes in contact with.

There have been times Monica has been in my home. You knew that in the early hours of the morning she was praying. You would wake up and feel the presence of the Lord in the entire house.

Thank you, Monica, for sharing what God has placed upon your heart to share. It has touched my heart and I know it will make a difference in the lives of others as they meditate on God's Word from you to them.

By Mrs. Jan Burkholder (She and her husband are Pastors of the New Covenant Assembly of God – Wiggins - Mississippi)

PRAYER

"My soul, hearken to the voice of your God. He is always ready to speak with you when you are prepared to hear. If there is any slowness to commune, it is not on His part but altogether on your own, for He stands at the door and knocks, and if His people will but open, He rejoices to enter."

Charles Haddon Spurgeon (1834-1892)

FOREWARD

To the readers of this significant and timely book, The End-Time Daughters of the King:

You are about to sit at the table to eat a very satisfying meal of spiritual food prepared by one of God's precious saints. Sister Monica Tomtania has sat at the feet of Jesus to listen and learn what the Spirit of the Lord is speaking to her and what He wants to reveal to His Church in these end times.

Monica is one of God's anointed ministers called to speak to the nations. I have personally been blessed by her teaching and ministry. She is a spiritual mother to many, a "mother in Israel", who has earned a platform to be heard. This maturity has come by years of serving God and serving others, through countless hours of prayer and by waiting at the feet of Jesus and by learning lessons taught by experiencing the depths of pain that comes with this life.

As you prayerfully read about the Biblical daughters of the King and of her life's experience in this book, you will be changed from the inside out and motivated to go to those He sends you.

Pastor Pat Chen, Founder and President
First Love Ministries International Prayer Center
"The Secret Place" Prayer Room Capitol Hill

"This is what the Lord says: "Restrain your voice from weeping, and your eyes from tears for your work will be rewarded," declares the Lord. "They will return from the land of the enemy. So there is hope for your future," declares the Lord. "Your children will return...." (Jeremiah 31:16-17).

PRAYERS

Spirit of the Living God, speak to us. Open us up. Make us willing to accept Your Word. Make our hearts and minds malleable to receive Your Word, to live Your Word, and to impact others with Your Word. In Christ name I pray.

A-men.

THE WORD OF THE LORD

"I will stand at my watch and station myself on the rampart; I will look to see what He will say to me, and what answer I am to give to this complaint. Then the Lord replied: "Write down the revelation and make it plain on tablets so that a herald may run with it. For the revelation awaits an appointed time; it speaks of the end and will not prove false. Though it lingers, wait for it; it will certainly come and will not delay."

(Habakkuk 2:1-3)

[1]

THE SPIRIT'S CRY

(It Is Time To Rise Up!)

"Arise, shine; for thy light is come, and the glory of the LORD is risen upon thee. For, behold, the darkness shall cover the earth, and gross darkness the people: but the LORD shall arise upon thee, and His glory shall be seen upon thee" (Isaiah 61:1-2).

"I am the LORD, and there is no other, apart from Me there is no God. I will strengthen you, though you have not acknowledged Me, so that from the rising of the sun to the place of its setting men may know there is none besides Me. I am the LORD, and there is no other" (Isaiah 45:5-6).

The Spirit's cry is being heard all over the world. He is creating urgency in the hearts of His people. The waters are being stirred up. He is calling out, who will listen? He is standing behind the doors saying, "Where are the Dorcases, who are willing to be My hand extended to the poor, the widow, and the outcast of society? Where are the Lydias, who will make their homes my habitation for the un-churched to find refuge? Where are all the Deborahs, who are zealous for Me, and would fight until they win the battle? Where are all the Miriams, who will usher My people into My presence with high praise and adoration? Where are the Annas, who will hear from Me and communicate My heart to all these hurting women all around them? Where are all the mighty women of valor?"

For over 15 years, I've been struck with unworthiness to convey this message to His daughters, although written and copyrighted since 2004. I wasn't ready to publish this message until July 2007, when I read an e-mail a friend sent to me with the prophecy from Kim Clement concerning women, which I quote:

> "...This sound is a sound of tenderness ... a sound of bold gentleness ... a sound has petrified the powers of hell, for this sound existed within Esther. The same sound existed in Deborah ... but the Spirit of God says 'they will arise, and when they arise, they will bring forth the Rock, Christ Jesus again!' ..... Women suddenly accelerating and touching the untouchable, and reaching the unreachable ... God says, "Tell these women, you are the instigators, and the initiators of the movement that is about to touch the entire earth. ..." (End of quote)

As we see the day approaching, thus the anointing the Lord is going to pour out on many women is going to increase tremendously. *"There is a mighty outpouring of great anointing already coming upon all classes, all races, and all colors of women world wide to ignite revival. The Holy Spirit is calling up a mighty army of women for this great move of God."* The Lord said to me.

This is the time! Rise up! Women of Zion! Your King is calling. His voice is sounding all around us. Wake up! For the Holy Spirit is ready for an outpouring of fire, of holiness, of grace, and of a mighty anointing over you. He is coming soon, and we are going up with a mighty army full of power and anointing! Jesus is coming soon.

You may think this book is not a great book as compared to the many you may have read before. It is neither sophisticated nor philosophical, but it is the Father's heart to you. It is written in its simplicity as given to me by the Holy Spirit. Please, I encourage you to pray and ask the Holy Spirit to create a hunger in you to take this message to heart. I pray the Holy Spirit will stir your heart to be a part of this great army of women the Lord is raising up for His own glory.

I am not perfect. I am only a willing imperfect vessel, carrying a message from the only Perfect Father (The King of this universe) to His daughters. Any error in this book may be strictly mine and not that of the Lord.

My Prayer

Father, help us to understand what You have to say to Your daughters today. Open our spiritual minds to comprehend the depth of this message. We are waiting. We long for Your return. We are crying for revival. Take us, break us, mold, us, refine us, and purify us. Take us where You want us to be, and rain down revival in our personal lives, and in the lands of our forefathers. Come, even so come, Holy Spirit of God. Let the fire of Your presence consume us, and set us lose to impact lives for Your glory. In the name of our Beloved Lord and Savior Jesus Christ, Amen.

THE WORD OF THE LORD

"Rise up! Thresh! Break into pieces, and proclaim the acceptable year of the Lord! Ride on with the King to victory. Your King is coming soon! He is coming with His rewards in His hands. Do not be afraid, I am with you. Do not be alarmed. I have called you. Lift up your head, strengthen the weak knees and thresh! Thresh! The Harvest is here. ..."

The KING of all kings!

(Eternally Self-Existent God–No Beginning and No End)

[2]

THE PROPHECY
(God Still Speaks!)

"For My thoughts are not your thoughts, neither are your ways My ways," declares the Lord. As the heavens are higher than the earth, so are My ways higher than your ways, and My thoughts than your thoughts. As the rain and the snow come down from heaven, and do not return to it without watering the earth and making it bud and flourish, so that it yields seed for the sower and bread for the eater, so is My Word that goes out from My mouth. It will not return to Me empty, but it will accomplish what I desire and achieve the purpose for which I sent it" (Isaiah 55: 8-11).

The Lord said to me. "I am raising up a mighty army of women — valiant women, warrior women, conquering women. I am raising them up from all walks of life into positions man has never dreamt of. They will invade the secular world. They will head governments, businesses ...as never before. But most important of all, I am elevating them to take positions in the Kingdom. They will lead My people, imparting knowledge, and direction. They are rising up from all walks of life; from every tribe and tongues, from all the corners of the world. They will be My mighty army of warriors that I am going to use to ignite revivals in the lands. They carry on their hearts and spirit deep wounds, and scars, bruises, and ashes of their past. I have refined them through the fires, and they carry my heart. I am taking them higher. They will lead many sons and daughters to the Kingdom. By their words, men will rise up to action. By their counsel, men will prevail in battles! ...

"Break Forth! Break through! Enlarge your tents, O daughters of the King. You will not be put to shame. The hour of your restoration has come. Rise up! Thresh! Break into pieces, and proclaim the acceptable year of the Lord! Ride on with the King to victory. Your King is coming soon! He is coming with His rewards in His hands. Do not be afraid, I am with you. Do not be alarmed. I have called you. Lift up your head, strengthen the weak knees and thresh! Thresh! The Harvest is here. ...

"Look! They are rising in the spirit of Deborah. They are rising up in the strength of Jael, and in the grace and humility of Ruth. They are armed like Esther, to dethrone kingdoms of evil, to promote My kingdom, and to bring down any stronghold that rises against the knowledge of God. ... They are rising up with mighty weapons. It is not with carnal weapons, but by My Spirit. My Spirit is upon them. My power will inundate them, and I will equip them for My glory. ....

"This is not man's doings. This is not a religion or a movement. It is My accomplishments for My Kingdom; by My Spirit. My zeal will bring My purposes on earth to pass. No human being can stop it ...."

"The word of the Lord came to me: "Son of man, the house of Israel is saying, 'The vision he sees is for many years from now, and he prophesies about the distant future.' Therefore say to them 'This is what the Sovereign Lord says. None of My words will be delayed any longer; whatever I say will be fulfilled, declares the Sovereign Lord" (Ezekiel 12:26-28).

(The Word of The Lord Given To Me In Togo - West Africa 1992)

PRAYERS

Lord, I thank You that Your Word is living and very active. It will never return to You void until it has accomplished what You purposed before the foundation of this world. You foresaw the restoration of women. You have foreseen our healing, our freedom, and our renewal. I am willing to be part of this great army You are raising up for Your glory. Give me a receptive mind, and a willing heart to be a vessel of honor for Your glory. In Jesus name I pray, a-men.

QUOTABLE QUOTES

"Christ is building His kingdom with earth's broken things. Men want only the strong, the successful, the victorious, the unbroken, in building their kingdoms; but God is the God of the unsuccessful, of those who have failed. Heaven is filling with earth's broken lives, and there is no bruised reed that Christ cannot take and restore to glorious blessedness and beauty. He can take the life crushed by pain or sorrow and make it into a harp whose music shall be all praise. He can lift earth's saddest failure up to heaven's glory."

James Russell Miller (1840-1912)

[3]

THE BEGINNING

(God Is About To Do Something New!)

❖

"This is what God the Lord says—He who created the heavens and stretched them out, who spread out the earth and all that comes out of it, who gives breath to its people, and life to those who walk on it. ... I will lead the blind by the ways they have not known, along unfamiliar paths I will guide them; I will turn the darkness into light before them and make the rough places smooth. These are things I will do; I will not forsake them" (Isaiah 42:5, 16)

Everything on this planet earth has a beginning. You will only appreciate the present when you remember where the Lord picked you from, and how far He has brought you. The wise King Solomon said,

> "To every thing there is a season, and a time to every purpose under the heaven: A time to be born and a time to die; a time to plant and a time to pluck that which was planted; ... a time to tear and a time to mend, a time to be silent and a time to speak. ... He hath made everything beautiful in His time: also He hath set the world in their heart, so that no man can find out the work that God maketh from the beginning to the end. ... I know that, whatsoever God doeth, it shall be forever: nothing can be put to it, nor anything taken from it; and God doeth it, that men should fear before Him. That which hath been is now; and that which is to be hath already been; and God requireth that which is past" (Ecclesiastes 3:1-2, 7, 11, 14-15).

HIS STORY (History)

Moses had journeyed with the children of Israel from Egypt to the plains of Moab. The Lord God instructed him to go to the top of Mount Nebo in Moab, across from Jericho, to view the land of Canaan, and be gathered to his ancestors, because he and Aaron did not uphold His holiness to honor His name before the people at Meribah. They permitted their anger and frustration to overrule the command of the Lord "to speak to the Rock." As you know, God does not play favorites. Then, and there, judgment fell. Moses' feet would not touch the Promised Land.

Moses was about to die. And the man, who had seen God, and talked to Him face to face, stood on the land of

Moab, on top of one of its mountains, to proclaim blessings over Israel.

> "...The Lord told Moses, "Go up into the Abarim Range to Mount Nebo in Moab, across from Jericho, and view Canaan, the land I am giving the Israelites as their own possession. There on the mountain that you have climbed you will die and be gathered to your people, just as your brother Aaron died on Mount Hor and was gathered to your people. This is because both of you broke faith with Me in the presence of the Israelites at the waters of Meribah Kadesh in the Desert of Zin and because you did not uphold My holiness among the Israelites. Therefore, you will see the land only from a distance; you will not enter the land I am giving to the people of Israel" (Deuteronomy 32:48-52).

Why did God choose the plains of Moab for Israel to encamp; for Joshua to be re-commissioned; and to prepare Moses for his death on Mount Moab or Nebo also known as Pisgah? Was it a coincidence? I don't think so, because there is no happenstance with God.

This is very interesting. Remember that the Moabites are Lot's descendants from his sexual relationship with his daughters as a result of his drunkenness (which may have brought a curse on Moab). However, there was a shifting in the spirit at that instant when Moses stood upon the Mount. His death and burial were symbolical, signifying to the world of a future prophetic transition from the Law to Grace. No man would understand it but God.

Moses' death was a picture of the "Death of the law" ushering in "Grace" through Joshua (Jesus – meaning Savior or Deliverer). When I say "Death of the Law," it does not imply that the Law was destroyed or abolished. It actually means that Grace came to give men the ability to obey the Law of God without falling dead right away. The Law of God is written on human hearts, giving them the ability to actually live the life of Christ, and finding forgiveness in failure, without being killed on the spot. The Law required immediate punishment and judgment on sin. But Grace gives man an opportunity to change or repent.

Moses' death was also symbolic of the cancellation of the curse placed upon Ruth's ancestors. Jesus, the Passover Lamb, which brought Israel out of the bondage of slavery, also broke the curse from Adam to today, opening the door for all Gentiles and Jew alike to find salvation through the saving knowledge of Jesus Christ.

Through this act of Moses' feet on Mount Pisgah in Moab, and the re-commissioning of Joshua to the ministry, God in His Sovereignty, in the realm of the spirit, reconnected to the descendants of Lot, who were representing the pagan world, by connecting them to the covenant God made with Abraham, *"In thee shall all the nations of the world be blessed."* Through this promise, the Lord began the process of bringing the Gentile world to Himself; and aligning His plan of redemption for all mankind even before Ruth was born.

Furthermore, the first converts, Rahab and her family, after the crossing of the Jordan, were pagans (Gentiles) saved by faith in the God of Israel by the scarlet thread, representing the blood of Christ. Rahab and her family were the first-fruits of the Gentile world, which came out with Joshua to inherit the promise land. Rahab married a man named Salmon, and bore Boaz, who became the kinsman redeemer and married Ruth. Was this an accident? You see, God is a God of order. Here begins the journey with the plan of redemption, and the coming revival through which Ruth became the fore-runner of Gentiles' betrothal to Christ.

Anyway, lest we forget, Joshua began his ministry with the miraculous crossing of the Jordan River. Then later on, Joshua led the children of Israel by the Word of the Lord, from victory to victory till they reached Canaan, and divided the land to all the tribes. The man Joshua is a type of our Lord Jesus Christ, who won the victory over satan, destroyed the stronghold of the enemy, and gave us eternal inheritance. Our Lord Jesus Christ "figuratively speaking" began His ministry with the Baptism of John the Baptist in the Jordan River, sanctioned with the Father's affirmation, and the confirmation of the Holy Spirit, *"This is My Beloved Son in who I am well-pleased."*

RECONNECTING THE LINK

In order to understand the depth of this message, it is imperative for us to start from the beginning to reconnect the dots. For it took the sacrifice of a family to bring about the beautiful story of Ruth, a forerunner through whom the Messiah came. Also, without the Elimelech family, the name of Ruth may not have been heard throughout all the Scriptures or elsewhere. Yet if we are enjoying the fruit of this great salvation our Lord brought to us, we must also remember that it took the death of three saints, and a dedicated young woman, to reconnect humanity to God's own sovereign plan of redemption, through the lineage of Judah.

The Elimelech family from the tribe of Judah had left their hometown Bethlehem of Judah because of famine. Israel had forsaken the Lord God who brought them out of the land of Egypt with a powerful outstretched hand against the Egyptians. Their problem was the fact that all the older generation who were supposed to teach their children about the living God, failed to do so. These fathers were now gone, and a new generation, who knew nothing about what the Lord did in bringing them in to the land of promise, rose up.

"The people served the Lord throughout the lifetime of Joshua and of the elders who outlived him and who had seen all the great things the Lord had done for Israel. After the whole generation had been gathered to their fathers, another generation grew up, who knew neither the Lord nor what He had done for Israel. Then the Israelites did evil in the eyes of the Lord and served the baals. They forsook the Lord, the God of their fathers, who had brought them out of Egypt. They followed various gods of the peoples around them. They provoked the Lord to anger because they forsook Him and served baal and the ashtoreths. In His anger against Israel, the Lord handed them over to raiders who plundered them...." (Judges 2:7, 10-15).

Most of them were not cognizant about the ways of God. So they turned quickly from the laws of God. As a result of their disobedience, God brought upon them all the curses He pronounced through His servant Moses concerning the abominations they were not to practice, and the consequences that would follow their disobedience. Please, you will do well to read the whole chapter.

"If you do not obey the Lord your God and do not carefully follow all his commands and decrees I am giving you today, all these curses will come upon you and overtake you: You will be cursed in the city and cursed in the country. Your basket and your kneading trough will be cursed... The Lord will cause you to be defeated before your enemies... You will plant a vineyard, but you will not even begin to enjoy its fruit. Your ox will be slaughtered before your eyes, but you will eat none of it. ... A people you do not know will eat what your land and your labor produce, and you will have nothing but cruel oppression all your days... You will sow much seed in the field but you will harvest little because locust will devour it ..." (Deuteronomy 28 NIV paraphrased).

According to the Scriptures, the Lord permitted their enemies to destroy their crops during harvest – hence Israel plunged into total suffering and famine. From time to time, God in His mercy raised up leaders (judges) to deliver them, judges like Gideon, Othniel, Deborah, Samson, Jephtae and the rest. It was in view of this cycle of suffering, that I believe, the hand of the Lord led the Elimelech family to Moab. Their ten-year stay in Moab, in men's eyes, yielded no fruit, for Elimelech's wife Naomi became the only survivor of the four that left Bethlehem. Naomi's comforters at that time were her daughters-in-law, who were bereaved themselves.

COMPARISON – PAST AND PRESENT GENERATION

A look at the generation of young people today and the decline of moral and Godly principles in the United States and the world at large, makes one consider the following critical questions: Do we evangelize other lands (which is good) but neglect our homelands? Have we become too rigid with religious rules of 'dos' and 'don'ts,', or do we presume that our children would know what they should automatically believe without being pointed to the Savior? Pathetically, some of us have not lived the Christ-like life before our children as salt and light. We preach the Word and live quite contrary to what we teach them.

Yes, the enemy has come into the garden secretly, because of our complacency, and has sown some bad seeds that are ruining the lives of this generation. The enemy's weeds have displaced the Truth, and choked up the seed of the Word in their hearts, because there were no spiritual mothers and fathers to nourish and guide them into maturity in the fear of the Lord.

The Body of Christ is to be blamed somehow for whatever is happening among our children today. We need to repent. We need to confess and ask for forgiveness. We need to live and portray to this generation the beauty of the Christ, who we say lives in us. They must see that we have been transformed by the power of His Spirit.

As I was weeping and praying for this nation, the Lord spoke to me in an audible voice. He said:

> "Monica, do not weep. I am raising up a mighty army of young men and young women, who have tasted the world and everything they desired, and have come to know that the answer is in serving Me alone. They will rise in the power of My Spirit, and defy the powers of darkness. Through them, I will bring revival into this land. They are rising up already, and nothing can stop them. It will be by My power, and by My Spirit, and not through any human means. They will break the power of denominationalism and dogmas, which has been hindering the full move of My Spirit in this nation these last days. They will move like giant locusts to invade the camp of the enemy with My power. I will blow them like trumpets to remind nations of My judgment, My grace and mercy, and use them for My own glory. I am preparing for Myself a bride no power can withstand ...." (2001).

Understand please, that according to the instructions given to the children of Israel in Psalms 78 through the intermediary of Moses, Israel was commanded to pass on the Word of the Lord to their children and the children's children. Here it goes.

"O my people, hear my teaching; listen to the words of my mouth. I will open my mouth in parables. I will utter hidden things, things from of old—what we have heard and known, what our fathers have told us. We will not hide them from their children; we will tell the next generation the praiseworthy deeds of the Lord, His power, and the wonders He has done. He decreed statutes for Jacob and established the law in Israel, which He commanded our forefathers to teach their children, so the next generation would know them, even the children yet to be born, and they in turn would tell their children. Then they would put their trust in God and would not forget His deeds, but would keep His commands. They would not be like forefathers—a stubborn and rebellious generations, whose hearts were not loyal to God, whose spirits were not faithful" (Psalms 78:1-8).

In summary, this was what the Lord commanded them to do.

- They should not hide God's precepts from their children.
- They should tell the next generation the praiseworthy deed of the Lord
- They should proclaim His power and the wonders He did in the past
- They should declare His Statutes and Laws, which He commanded our fathers to obey.

Why were they commanded to mentor their generation? And why do we also need to mentor this vulnerable generation? The answer is clearly stated in the Scriptures:

- So the next generation will know God's Word.
- The children yet to be born shall know them because we passed on the torch.
- They in turn would tell their children. It will be a generational-pass-on-blessing.
- They would put their trust in God and not in their own achievements or any other things.
- They would not forget His deeds (works).
- They would keep His commands.
- They would not be like others in the past – hardhearted, stubborn, rebellious and ungrateful.
- Their hearts would be loyal and faithful to the Lord.
- They will not willfully put God to the test.
- They will not speak against God.
- They will not end their days in premature deaths.
- They will not rebel and be destroyed by God.
- They will remember that God is their Rock.
- They will remember that the Lord is their Redeemer and Savior.

And the result will be: That the Lord will not abandon them, and they will be blessed by the Lord. I believe God requires us to follow His commands to Moses. We need to heed these admonitions from the heart of our Heavenly Father.

The Word of God says: *"My people are destroyed from lack of knowledge ...."* (Hosea 4:6). What is the meaning of this Scripture? I am not a Bible Scholar. I am just a called handmaiden of the Lord, but I have been to the College of the Holy Ghost. All the textbooks in this College were written by Him. He is with me all the time to give me more clarification of His written Word. And since I needed clarification of this particular verse, I talked to my Professor. He is always there to teach, and to remind me of everything I might forget during His class session. Professor Holy Ghost spoke to me and said: *"Monica, where there is no clarity of divine guidance, the people go astray."* When people have not received clear guidance and understanding from the Spirit of the Lord through the teaching of His Word, through divine revelation, they actually follow wrong paths, and listen to deceptive voices.

GOD'S INTERVENTION

The Lord God knew that in His plan of salvation for the entire human race including both the Jew and the Gentile, He would need mixed instruments through which He would perfect His ultimate purpose for mankind. So in order for His purposes to be fulfilled, God led the Elimelech family into a pagan land called Moab. I say God led this family, because nothing happens to a child of God without the knowledge of this Almighty God. We can look back into the story of Joseph in Egypt, which eventually led all of Jacob's family to land in Egypt. It was not a coincidence, for the Lord had promised Abraham that his descendants would go through Egypt. Someone had to lead the way. Someone needed to pay the price, and someone must be the sacrifice.

> "Then the Lord said to Abram, 'Know for certain that your descendants will be strangers in a country not their own, and they will be enslaved and mistreated four hundred years. But I will punish the nation they serve as slaves and afterward they will come out with great possession" (Genesis 15:13-14).

Although the story of this family has been preached many times in the negative sense, we need to understand that nothing happens to any child of God devoid of His knowledge. Anything that happens to a child of God has a purpose, which God will ultimately work out for His own glory.

The King of glory needed the black and white keys of the piano of humanity (the Jew and the Gentile, male and female) to blend together to play the perfect symphony (music) of the birth of His Only begotten Son – the Savior of mankind. God needed that accord. But it was only going to spring up when a seed died. Do you remember what Jesus said concerning His death? He said:

> "Unless a kernel of wheat falls to the ground and dies it remains only a single seed. But if it dies, it produces many seeds" (John 12:24).

Notice the expression **"a kernel,"** which denotes **a single seed.** In other words, it can read, "When a single seed falls to the ground and dies, it yields more than one fruit."

This reminds me of some special peppers in Africa called 'bird's eye' peppers. They are very small but hotter than the normal jalapenos. Birds grow these peppers. Our people dry normal peppers in an open space during pepper season. Birds fly by and eat these peppers, and thereby plant the peppers seeds through their feces. The most amazing thing is that the seeds of the former peppers they eat are not as hot as the ones they plant. The latter is extremely hot. This is inconceivable, but this is exactly what happens when the death of a seed occurs. It yields more than the normal one seed, and it becomes 'stronger and powerful' than before. One seed yields lots of grains. A cup of corn yields sacks of corn. John Henry Jowett wrote,

> "Death is not the end; it is only a new beginning. Death is not the master of the house; he is only the porter at the King's lodge, appointed to open the gate and let the King's guest in to the realm of the eternal."

It took three seeds or three kernels' death, that is, Elimelech, Mahlon and Chilion, to prepare the ground for the Messianic Seed to spring up. It took the death of three men, a typology of God the Father, God the Son, and God the Holy Spirit to unify and complete the plan of salvation for humanity; that is for the whole world to experience the gift of salvation.

The Triune God lowered Himself to come to a world that was void of the bread of Life, to a people that have rejected Him to save them from their iniquities. Christ's death has brought about millions of souls delivered from the power of darkness, from satan's grip, marching on to the Glory Land. What a wonder!

A MYSTERY TO GOD?

The death of these three wasn't pleasant and bearable to Naomi and her daughters-in-law. No one could understand the misfortune of this family, but the Lord knew it all before it ever happened. He is all knowing and does not consult anyone before He does His bidding. He is Almighty and the only Sovereign Lord.

> "Who hath measured the waters in the hollow of His hand, and meted out the heaven with the span, and comprehended the dust of the earth in a measure, and weighed the mountains in scales, and the hills in a balance? Who hath directed the Spirit of the Lord, or being His counselor hath taught Him? With who took He counsel, and who instructed Him, and taught Him in the path of judgment, and taught Him knowledge, and showed to Him the way of understanding?" (Isaiah 40:12-14).

To emphasize this, these two young men and their father one more time, represent God the Father, who begot Jesus Christ our Savior, then sent the indwelling and the endowment of the Holy Spirit on all who believe. These Three (Triune God), yet One, consented right from the beginning of creation to share Their life and nature in creating man after Their Likeness.

"And God said, 'Let Us make man in Our image, in Our likeness, and let them rule over the fish of the sea and the birds of the air, over the livestock, over all the earth, and over all the creations that move along the ground.' So God created man in His own image, in the image of God He created him; male and female He created them" (Genesis 1:26-27).

And after the fall, this same Triune God went every mile in search of man to bring him back into having a relationship with Him.

When we take a close look at the annunciation of the birth of Christ, we see the Trinity in action, preparing to lay Himself bare at the mercy of us carnal, selfish, and sinful beings in order to buy us back from the enemy. Also throughout the ministry of Christ, we observe the witness of all Three in operation until the day the Perfect Sacrifice was offered to redeem us all. Oh what Love! Oh what a sacrifice!

* * * * * * *

We cannot remove the death of these three individuals from God's plan of action in bringing salvation to all mankind. Without their death, Naomi and Ruth would not have gone back to Israel. Furthermore, without the sacrifice, the determination and the obedience of Ruth to follow the leadings of God for her life, God's plan may have been interrupted. Elimelech, Mahlon, and Chilion's death was somehow an inexplicable sacrifice for all mankind, leading them to Christ Jesus, the Perfect Sacrifice for Jews and Gentiles alike.

LIMITED UNDERSTANDING

I remember the day in the year 2000, when the Lord spoke to me about how He was going to honor my husband. In my finite mind, I figured out how it was going to be. I knew He had already spoken to me to leave Togo in 1992, and so I thought our moving out of Togo and resigning from Calvary Temple, and the way the Church was going to honor us was what the Lord was talking about. Even when He started revealing the death of Geoffrey to me in 1999, I fought over it, fasted and prayed, canceled the spirit of death, broke all the powers of darkness I could break in order to divert death in our family. I stood on the Word of the Lord in Psalms 91:16 repeatedly saying 'No and No' to death, and claimed long life for my darling.

Regardless of all the health food I cooked, despite all the vegetable juices I made, despite six months of having all-night prayer meetings every day, and fasting at least three days within the week, standing on the promises of God, Geoffrey's health continued to go downhill. Despite the long hours of refusing to release Geoffrey, when he was begging me like a child, to allow him to enter the presence of the Lord, while the angels were lingering around, He took Geoffrey away. I thought in my head, *"This is unfair. He is young. He is only 54."* I could not understand the reason.

Now when he passed away, I saw the thousands of people who came to the funeral and I heard, and read great testimonies coming from around the world. Although I was crying, not believing what had happened to my children and me, the still small voice of the Lord whispered to my heart again saying,

> "Monica, I have honored Geoffrey on earth, and the greater one is yet to come, when I shall sit with all of you in glory to proclaim Geoffrey's faithfulness, love and consecration to Me. I have honored him because I came Myself to welcome Him home and left that testimony on earth to you, the children, and the church. I have honored him because many have come to know Me through his suffering, and his homecoming. ..."

Beloved child of God, you may be hard-pressed and in a difficult situation right now; you may be at your wits-end not knowing where help will come from, you may not understand why the Lord has allowed all these 'evils' to come upon you and your family, but I have good news for you. GOD IS IN CONTROL! Nothing falls dead without His knowledge! A dead seed in God's hand is worth more than a million unprofitable living ones! What He demands is faithfulness and determination to see the end result in God's own way.

CONSTANT HUNGER AND DEEP CRAVINGS

There was nothing said about the Elimelech family turning to the gods of the land of Moab. The Bible is silent about it; however, it mentions what led them to Moab. Hunger drove them into this foreign land, which only knew of small gods and superstitions. But their desperation for natural food led them to win a soul for the God of Israel, who in turn brought blessings to the whole world.

Do you know why many of us have such a craving for natural food or a problem with bulimia, anorexia and the rest? A lot of people may not know this, and doctors may diagnose something else; but oftentimes, intense physical hunger for natural food or even lack of it has a spiritual connection. It denotes a lack of some spiritual nutrients in our day-to-day walk with the Lord. Hunger for more food, even when we know we are not hungry, indicates a spiritual hunger for something greater in the spirit realm, which needs attention. It is the wooing of the Spirit of God. He wants to fill all the potholes in our lives. He wants to take us into a deeper and a higher realm of His presence, so that we can be a blessing to someone else. Jesus said, *"Blessed are those who hunger and thirst after righteousness, for they will be filled" (Matthew 5:6).*

Desperate to find satisfaction in life, and crying for help with prayer and fasting, the Lord gave me this song.

> Let the Fire, the Pentecostal Fire
> Keep burning in my soul
> Let the Power, the Holy Spirit's Fire
> Keep burning in my soul
> Fill the vacuum in my soul
> Fill the potholes in my life
> Set the chaffs in flames
> And let the fire keep burning

I found this secret in my walk with the Lord. The less I read the Bible and pray, the more intense my hunger for natural or unnecessary food becomes. On the other hand, during the times that I spend more time with the Lord through prayer and the reading of the Word, the fewer cravings I have for unnecessary food. His presence fills me up. And time and again, I just want to be left alone. Eating at that time becomes somewhat of a chore to me.

GOD IS IN CONTROL

Elimelech and his family, I believe, were faithful to the Lord, which we will see later on in the message, because their faith had an impact on Ruth. Just ten years of living in Moab made a record in the history of humanity forever.

The Elimelech family's dedication to the Lord might have been exceptional at a time when Israel was battling with infidelity, lawlessness, idolatry, wars, and famines. I believe they could not stand whatever was happening in Israel at that time, and also knew that leaving their people (family) to a foreign land could be very expensive to their spiritual and moral lives; yet they did make the move.

Many times you may be moved by the Spirit of the Lord to make certain decisions, which to men may sound foolish and detrimental to the lives of your family, however when it is orchestrated by an unseen hand, there is nothing one can do about it. Yes, there is nothing to fear when He is the Orchestrator.

Why would the Lord tell us to go to California when my husband was sick, when He knew Geoffrey wasn't going to live? Why did He ask me to leave the country of Togo after serving the Women's Ministry for fifteen good years as national director? What honor and remuneration did we get after laboring in Togo, especially Calvary Temple all these years? Why should I come and suffer in the United States with no help from anywhere, and grieving among people who knew little about who I was, and what the Lord has brought me through? Why are some members of the Christian community and some pastors very hostile and prejudiced against immigrants in a nation that calls itself 'Christian' nation?

These are just a few questions I have asked myself over and over. I am just expressing an overall view, not individual efforts to make my stay comfortable. I do not have all the answers, and He has not given me an answer yet, but I know God has a purpose in everything that we may be going through today. He will one day make it clear.

If Naomi were here today, she might have told me she did not know what led her and her husband, and her two children to go to Moab. She would, maybe, tell me she did not understand why the Lord deprived her of her family, but she can now conclude saying: "It was worth it to become the great grandmother of our Lord and Savior Jesus Christ!" What a beautiful picture! What a happy ending!

QUOTABLE QUOTES

"Jesus never sends a man ahead alone. He blazes a clear way through every thicket and woods, and then softly calls, "Follow Me. Let's go on together, you and I." He has been everywhere we are called to go. His feet have trodden down smooth a path through every experience that comes to us. He knows each road, and knows it well: the valley road of disappointment with its dark shadows; the steep path of temptation down through the rocky ravines and slippery gullies; the narrow path of pain, with the brambly thorn bushes so close on each side, with their slash and sting; the dizzy road along the heights of victory; the old beaten road of common-place daily routine. Everyday paths He has trodden and glorified, and will walk anew with each of us. The only safe way to travel is with Him alongside and in control."

Dr. Samuel Dickey Gordon (1859-1936)

[4]

LET'S TELL HER STORY
(We All Have A Story!)

❖

"The God who made the world and everything in it is the Lord of heaven and earth and does not live in temples built by hands. And He is not served by human hands, as if He needed anything, because He Himself gives all men life and breath and everything else. From one man He made every nation of men, that they should inhabit the whole earth; and He determined the times set for them and the exact places where they should live. God did this so that men would seek after Him and perhaps reach out for Him and find Him, though He is not far from each one of us. 'For in Him we live and move and have out being.' ...

(Acts 17: 24-28).

The beginning of Ruth's story started as a young Moabitish girl, whose family history was not pleasant to hear. Her family history was tainted with greed, idolatry, immorality, incest, and superstitions, but it is also filled with God's amazing grace.

Ruth was raised up as a Moabitish young girl who only knew the worship of the gods of wood, silver, and gold. But one day, her destiny changed, when she met a Jewish young man, who had a covenant with the living God. Ruth's future was going to be shaped, because she entered into a relationship with a family, who was not ordinary. This family had a covenant with the Lord Jehovah, for they were descendants of the tribe of the Lion of Judah.

If you know your Bible very well, you may have read the story of a man named Lot. He was the nephew of Abraham. When the Lord God called Abraham out of the land of the Chaldeans to leave his people and go to a land He was going to show him, he took his nephew Lot, with him. And the story continues to tell us how because of Abraham, the Lord blessed Lot also, for the Bible states in the Book of Genesis, that Lot had great possessions just like Abraham, because he was in covenant with Abraham's God. And Abraham's blessings or anointing also came upon Lot, as a direct result of his association with Abraham. We are blessed to be a blessing!

> "And Lot also, which went with Abraham, had flocks, and herds, and tents" (Genesis 13:5).

One day, a conflict arose between the servants of Lot and those of Abraham, because of their possessions. To make a long story short, Abraham and Lot separated. Lot went ahead straight into Sodom and Gomorrah, a land filled with all kinds of vices (Genesis 13:5-13). The Bible tells us the people in Sodom and Gomorrah were homosexuals and immoral to such a point, they even wanted to have sex with the angels God had sent to destroy the city.

"Before they had gone to bed, all the men from every part of the city of Sodom – both young and old – surrounded the house. They called out to Lot, "Where are the men who came to you tonight? *Bring them out to us so that we can have sex with them."*

Were these people created to be homosexuals, lesbians, or bi-sexual? Obviously not! If they were, God would not have destroyed them. Although God still loves sinners, He hates the iniquities people have deliberately chosen to thwart His plans and purposes for mankind regarding the sanctity of marriage. You see, any lifestyle that goes against the Word of God, attracts God's judgment.

"The wrath of God is being revealed from heaven against all the godlessness and wickedness of men who suppress the truth by their wickedness, since what may be known about God is plain to them, because God has made it plain to them. For since the creation of the world God's invisible qualities—His eternal power and divine nature—have been clearly seen, being understood from what has been made, so that men are without excuse. For although they knew God, they neither glorified Him as God nor gave thanks to Him, but their thinking became futile and their foolish hearts darkened. Although they claimed to be wise, they became fools and exchanged the glory of the immortal God for images ..... Therefore God gave them over in the sinful desires of their hearts to sexual impurity for the degrading of their bodies with one another. They exchanged the truth of God for a lie, and worshiped and served created things rather than the Creator—who is forever praised. Amen. Because of this, God gave them over to shameful lusts. Even their women exchanged natural relations for unnatural ones. In the same way the men also abandoned natural relations with women and were inflated with lust for one another. Men committed indecent acts inflamed with lust for one another, and received in themselves the due penalty for their perversion. Furthermore, since they did not think it worthwhile to retain the knowledge of God, He gave them over to a depraved mind, to do what ought not to be done. They have become filled with every kind of wickedness, evil, greed and depravity. They are full of envy, murder, strife, deceit and malice. They are gossipers, slanderers, God haters, insolent, arrogant and boastful; they are senseless, faithless, heartless, ruthless. Although they know God's righteous decree that those who do such things deserve death, they not only continue to do these very things but also approve of those who practice them" (Romans 1:18-32).

We need to love sinners, and still be willing to tell them the truth of God's unconditional love and judgment with compassion, and if possible, with tears to drag them out of hell.

Now, look at this scenario; the men of Sodom thought the angels were ordinary human beings. Although Lot offered his daughters to them, they were so blinded they wanted rather to sleep with the angels.

"Lot went outside to meet them and shut the door behind him and said, 'No, my friends. Don't do this wicked thing. I have two daughters who have never slept with a man. Let me bring them out to you, and you can do what you like with them. But don't do anything to these men, for they have come under the protection of my roof" (Gen 19:4-8 – emphasis mine).

God's verdict fell for destruction. Before the city was destroyed, the grace of God brought Lot and his family out, although he was hesitant.

"With the coming of dawn, the angels urged Lot, saying: 'Hurry! Take your wife and your two daughters who are here, or you will be swept away when the city is punished.' When he hesitated, the men grasped his hand and the hands of his wife and of his two daughters and led them safely out of the city, for the Lord was merciful to them" (Genesis 19:15-16).

GOD IS CALLING!

Precious daughters of God, the still small voice of the Lord is calling you and me out of this world's system into a deeper relationship with Him. What is holding you from running away from the presence of sin, which is snaring you to fall into the enemy's destruction? We cannot hold on to the lifestyle of Sodom and still enjoy the presence of the Lord. We cannot remain in a sinful environment, involvement, and pollutions, and still maintain a good relationship with the God of perfect purity (holiness). The Bible says:

"Ye adulterers and adulteresses, know ye not that the friendship of the world is enmity with God? Whoever therefore will be a friend of the world is the enemy of God" (James 4:4).
"Love not the world, neither the things that are in the world. If any man loves the world, the love of the Father is not in him. For all that are in the world, the lust of the flesh, the lust of the eyes and the pride of

life, is not of the Father, but of the world. The world passes away, and the lust thereof, but he that doeth the will of God abides for ever" (I John 2:15-17).

He is calling out His Bride from the world's system into a higher realm of His infinite love and mercy. We have no time to waste. The command has been given: "Hurry! Or you will be swept away!" (Genesis 19:15).

Since the Lord wanted to give Lot and his family another chance of going into His presence and enjoying the covenant because of Abraham his uncle, He gave him the command to flee to the mountains; yet, Lot wasn't willing to take any risk.

"As soon as they brought them out, one of them said: "Flee for your lives! Don't look back, and do not stop any where in the plains! Flee to the mountains or you will be swept away!" (Genesis 19:17).

Grace has brought us out of our Sodom and Gomorrah. Yet the Lord has entrusted the rest of our walk with Him into our hands in the daily choices we make. We are not robots to be controlled with machines. God has given us wills and desires, empowered by His Spirit, to help us make right decisions. What we do with that opportunity is up to us. All He wants is our collaboration with Him to perfect us according to His plans and purposes. He is admonishing us together with the Lot family to follow these four instructions in order to survive in this wicked and crooked generation.

- **Flee for our lives.** "Flee from all appearances of evil" (1 Thessalonians 5:22). "We want each of you to show the same diligence to the very end, in order to make your hope sure" (Hebrews 6:11).

- **No need looking back.** The moment we gave our lives to the Lord, we signed a contract never ever to look back. *"Anyone who puts his (her) hand to the plow and looks back is not fit for the kingdom of God"* (Luke 8:62 – emphasis mine).
- **Do not stop anywhere in the plains.** There is no need to be sluggish or stagnant. *"Desire the sincere milk of the Word, whereby you may grow....."* (I Peter 2:1-2). *"Forgetting those things which are behind, and reaching forth unto those things which are before us. I press toward the mark for the prize..."* (Philippians 3:13-14).
- **Flee to the mountains.** Flee to the presence of the Lord. King David said, *"I will lift up mine eyes to the hills (mountains)—where does my help come from the Lord, the Maker of heaven and earth"* (Psalms 12:1-2). *"Who may ascend the hills of the Lord? Who may stand in His Holy place? He who has clean hands, and a pure heart; who does not lift up his soul to an idol or swear by what is false. He will receive blessings from the Lord and vindication from God his savior"* (Psalms 24:3-5). In the Lord's presence we gain strength to live a holy life. *"Thou will show me the path of life: In Thy presence is fullness of joy, at Thy right hand there are pleasures for ever more"* (Psalms 16:11).

In God's mercy, He wanted Lot and his family to run to the mountain for renewal, for spiritual and emotional healing; for a refreshing after the shock; and for restoration after their loss. Mountains sometimes describe obstacles. But in the Bible, the mountain also depicts God's dwelling place or His Holy presence. Do you remember God speaking to Moses on the mountain?

"Lord who shall abide in thy tabernacle? Who shall dwell in thy holy hill? ......" (Psalms 15:1). Please, you can also read the entire Psalm.

"Who shall ascend into the hill of the Lord? Or who shall stand in His holy hill? He that hath clean hands and a pure heart; who hath not lifted up his soul to vanity, nor sworn deceitfully.... He shall receive the blessing from the Lord and righteousness from the God of his salvation" (Ps 24:3-5).

The Lord wanted Lot to experience the blessings of His presence, which he enjoyed when he was with Abraham. He wanted Lot to go back into covenant with Him because of Abraham. Lot was described in the Bible as a righteous man because of his faith in Jehovah God, and one who was in constant battle with the evil of Sodom, according to the book of II Peter 2:6-9.

"And turning the cities of Sodom and Gomorrah into ashes condemned them with an overthrow, making them an example unto those that after should live ungodly; and delivered just Lot, vexed with the filthy conversation of the wicked: (For that righteous man dwelling among them, in seeing and hearing, vexed his righteous soul from day to day with their unlawful deeds)..."

Since Sodom's environment had paralyzed Lot's heart, he could not sacrifice to go higher into the presence of the Lord. Lot argued his way out of God's infinite mercy to bring him closer again into deeper fellowship with Him on His holy hill (mountain).

The Lord doesn't condone our compromises, but His permissive will and mercy sometimes, permit us to make our own choices, and wait to see us reaping the harvest of our own demise. We all have the tendency to push God around like a robot, and to mold Him into our own ways and plans.

EXCUSES AND EXCUSES

There were three men who came to Jesus and offered to follow Him. However, all three of them had some excuses and certain things to care for before following the Lord fully.

"As they were walking along the road, a man said to him, "Lord, I will follow you wherever you go." Jesus replied, "Foxes have holes and birds of the air have nests, but the Son of man has no place to lay His head." He said to another man, "Follow me." But the man replied, "**Lord, first let me go and bury my father.**" Jesus said to him, "Let the dead bury their own dead, but you go and proclaim the Kingdom of God."
Still another said, "I will follow you, Lord, but **first let me go back and say good-by to my family.**" Jesus replied, "No man having put his hand to the plow, and looks back is fit for service in the kingdom" (Luke 9:57-62 NIV).

There is a great price we must pay for being His disciples, and we are not exempt from such sacrifice. Grace demands even more — Grace demands total consecration (Luke 14:26-34).

* * * * * * *

Lot became somehow complacent as he continued to stay in Sodom, and maybe could not discern between the will of God and that of his own. He did not have a vision. He was short sighted, even though he knew what the will of the Lord was, for the Bible says, *"Where there is no vision the people perish."* Lot had become, in some way, indifferent and desensitized as a result of being exposed for a long time to evil, and he limited the Lord's ability to take him to the mountains. He said, *"... But I can't flee to the mountain, this disaster will overtake me, and I'll die" (Genesis 19:19).*

Wasn't the grace that was bringing him out of Sodom sufficient enough to take him to the mountains? Lot wanted to land in another place he was familiar with, but that city was as filthy and sinful as Sodom and Gomorrah. The angels were about to destroy that city too; but when Lot demanded to land there, the angels agreed to his petition and spared the land of Zoar. This is the way we normally limit God. I have done that many times.

> "Lot said to them, "... But I can't flee to the mountain; this disaster will overtake me and I'll die. Look, here is a town near enough to run to, and it is small. Let me flee to it – it is very small, isn't it? Then my life will be spared" (Gen 19:19-20).

SIN – A DANGEROUS COMPANION

When sin is not totally dealt with, as commanded by the Lord, it always raises up its ugly head much stronger than it was before. The Lord Jesus made a remark with reference to the demon (an unclean spirit) that leaves a house (the human soul).

> "When an unclean spirit is gone out of a man, he walks through dry places, seeking rest, and finding none. Then he says, "I will return into my house from whence I came out"; and when he is come, he finds it empty, and garnished. Then he goes and takes with

himself seven other spirits more wicked than himself, and enter in and dwell there. And the last state of that man is worse than the first. Even so shall it be also unto this wicked generation" (Matthew 12: 43-44).

The same sin of homosexuality and immorality, which was not destroyed because of Lot's fear and compromise, has now come forth in full force destroying this generation. If Zoar had been destroyed with Sodom and Gomorrah, who knows what would have become our world today. Had it been that Lot had gone to the mountain as instructed earlier by the angels, it may have been a different story for our world today. *"Watch out for the little compromises that destroy one's future,"* says King Solomon.

"Catch for us the foxes, the little foxes that ruin the vineyards, our vines that are in bloom" (Song of Songs 2:15).

It takes the power of His presence to break down those strongholds of little foxes in one's life. The power of the Lord to overcome all other potential temptations, to break all the garbage strongholds he collected from Sodom, was in His holy presence – over the mountain; for the presence of the Lord transforms. Yet he did not want to go there because he was afraid just like the children of Israel, who were also afraid to hear the Lord speak to them directly during the time of Moses.

When Moses went to the presence of the Lord over the mountain, the Bible says his countenance was changed completely. The people of Israel could not look upon him. Moses met God face to face (Exodus 34:29-35).

Friends, the presence of the Lord brings deliverance. The presence of the Lord renders one clean. The presence of the Lord brings down the glory of God.

* * * * * * *

Lot and His family, I believe, left the city without anything. The moment they left, God rained fire and brimstone on Sodom and Gomorrah. The riches, which brought dispute between him and his uncle, Abraham, were now burning in the fire of God's wrath. Mrs. Lot could not stand to see her riches under fire. She wanted to look at the backdrop just for a little time. She did not make it to their final destination over in Zoar, and became a pillar of salt because she did not obey the command of the Lord not to look back.

"And it came to pass, when they have brought them forth abroad, that he said, 'Escape for your life: look not behind thee, neither stay thou in the plain; escape to the mountain, lest thou be consumed.' ...... And his wife looked back from behind him and she became a pillar of salt" (Gen 19:17, 26).

The command was given, "Do not look back". Why look back? The answer is that although she left Sodom, her heart was still there. Pathetic! She perished for disobeying God's command. The Bible clearly states in 1 John 2:15-17,

"Do not love the world or anything in the world. If anyone loves the world, the love of the Father is not in him. For everything in the world—the craving of sinful man, the lust of his own eyes and the boasting of what he has and does—comes not from the Father but from the world. The world and its desires pass away, but the man who does the will of God lives forever."

We have all received a command from the Lord to turn our backs to the 'world.' The very day you and I gave our lives to the Lord, we signed a contract with Him as said earlier. There are lots of implications in this contract (to be discussed later in the book) we need to heed or else we can never be a part of this end-time revival the Holy Spirit is preparing at the coming of the Lord. God the Father signed this contract with the blood of the Lamb – Jesus Christ, God the Son, and the witness was the Holy Spirit. You do well never ever to break this contract. For it was very, very expensive.

WATCH OUT!

From the day Lot's wife looked back, all her descendants also turned their back against the Lord God Jehovah, Abraham had introduced them to, into a lifestyles of superstitions, idolatry, and paganism they were taken from, starting from her own children. Jesus, giving a warning about the end-time referred to Lot's wife.

"Remember Lot's wife" (Luke 17:32).

We must understand that whatever decisions and choices we made in the past, and are making today will affect our children and others who saw us making such decisions around us. When we walk away from the Lord for just a single moment or a few hours for worldly pleasures and enjoyment, we lose a whole generation of those who look up to us for inspiration.

Holy living or Godly choices are very expensive and sacrificial, but very beneficial. Although you may suffer ridicule, persecution, and all kinds of evil against you in the beginning, you will harvest the fruit of your righteous living with many blessings in the end, with the joy of the Lord, ringing in your soul.

Joseph's refusal to sleep with Potiphar's wife, landed him in prison, but in the end, his faithfulness was rewarded. He became the Prime Minister of Egypt. Please read Genesis 39:7-23.

THE PATHETIC STORY

Now, here comes the miserable and pathetic story of the beginning of the Moabites. Lot and the two daughters arrived at Zoar tired, exhausted and lonely. They were somehow complete strangers in the land of their own choice. And according to the confession of the daughters, it seemed there were no men in the plain of Zoar. It may be true! Or they might have schemed or designed it to commit incest with their father. Who knows what would have happened had their mother obeyed the commandment of the Lord.

As soon as they arrived, the first thing that came into the mind of these girls was to practice what they had seen others do in Sodom and Gomorrah – incest. This was not even orchestrated by Lot but by the girls. Do you see the picture here? And both had children with their drunken father.

"And Lot went up out of Zoar and dwelt in the mountain and his two daughters with him; for he feared to dwell in Zoar and he dwelt in a cave, he and his daughters. And the first born said unto the younger, 'Our father is old, and there is not a man in the earth to come in unto us after the manner of all the earth: Come Let us make our father drink wine, and we will lie with him, that we may preserve seed of our father.' And they made their father drink wine that night; and the firstborn went in, and lay with her father; and he perceived not when she lay down, nor when she arose. ……..and the younger arose and lay with him….. Thus were both the daughters of Lot with child by their father. And the firstborn bare a son, and called his name Moab.... And the younger bare a son and called him Ben-am'-mi (Amorites) ..." (Gen 19:30-38).

Anyway, Moab in Hebrew is **'Mowab'** meaning "From my father", and **'Ben-am'-mi'** also means, 'Son of my people'. Doesn't it sound strange? Obviously! It is more likely the daughters also became corrupted in their mind by the standard of living and lifestyle of Sodom and Gomorrah. We are all prone to sin. We stand firm today because of His grace alone.

Sexual immoral and perverse people do not know the difference between a family member and a stranger. Fornication and adultery is not regarded as sinful to our secular world; yet it is a real problem today in this generation, and God does not approve it. Pornography, stealing, lying, incest, immorality, lawlessness, and all kinds of vices have become rampant. Why? It is because the media is publicizing it everyday as normal lifestyle, and our children watch it being demonstrated in films and et cetera. This is the reason the Bible clearly warns us concerning evil communications or ungodly companions.

> "Do not be misled: Bad company corrupts good character. Come back to your senses as you ought to, and stop sinning; for there are some who are ignorant of God ...." (I Corinthians 15:33-34).

> "Do not be deceived: God is not mocked. A man reaps what he sows. The one who sows to please his/her sinful nature, from that nature will reap destruction ..." Galatians 6:7-8).

Whatever lifestyle Lot's girls were exposed to, was copied somehow precisely by the girls from Sodom. Sodom and Gomorrah's immoral practice was exactly what they put into action, and the first incest was recorded in the Bible. Look at how wild the fire of sin is. Once it finds a root, it spreads out rapidly to destroy thousands of lives and properties. One act of Sodomy has polluted the whole world and is destroying our society today. One act of incest flung the door wide open for more like cankerworms. Examples:

- Reuben slept with his father's wife, Bilhah (Genesis 35:22, 49:4).
- Judah committed incest with his daughter in law Tamar, when she played the harlot (Genesis 38: 16-18).
- Amnon raped his own sister Tamar (II Samuel 13:1-14).
- Absalom slept with his father's wives (II Samuel 16:2).
- Herod took his brother, Phillip's wife, and killed John the Baptist for reproving him. (Matthew 14:3-4).
- In the Corinthian church, someone was sleeping with his father's wife. Paul admonished them to remove such a one from the congregation (I Corinthians 5).

The Bible is not silent on this subject, neither does it agree with these wicked and immoral lifestyles. The Lord sounds a serious warning against such practices. All these practices are called immorality, lawlessness, and wickedness, which is punishable through hell fire, if not confessed, denounced, and abandoned.

"Do you not know that the wicked will not inherit the kingdom of God? Do not be deceived: Neither the sexually immoral nor idolaters nor adulterers nor male prostitutes nor homosexual offenders nor thieves nor the greedy nor drunkards nor slanderers nor swindlers will inherit the kingdom of God" (I Corinth 6:9-10).

* * * * * * *

Going back to our story and tracing through biblical history of the Moabites, we get a glimpse of the background of the Moabites, from whom Ruth emerged. First of all, they had a shameful past including incest and sexual sins. Secondly, they were cursed, and excluded or banned from entering into the congregation of the people of God. They actually became Israel's perpetual enemies according to the Word of the Lord.

"An Ammonite or Moabite shall not enter into the congregation of the Lord; even to their tenth generation shall they not enter into the congregation of the Lord forever... **Thou shall not seek their peace nor their prosperity all thy days for ever**" (Deut 23:3, 6 – emphasis mine).

A DIVINE TURN AROUND

Nevertheless, by divine appointment, Ruth went from a shameful past into becoming a part of God's chosen people. Ruth's choice to marry or be a part of Elimelech's family made her a candidate for the blessings of Abraham. Ruth's preference to leave her family after the death of her husband to follow after Naomi broke the curse of generational bondages of infidelity, instability, and sexual sin of incest. Her confessions of faith in Jehovah God, and her confidence in His wounded handmaiden Naomi, opened the door for the full plan of God to be unfolded into her destiny.

Ruth's chosen lifestyle of total abandonment, humility, submission, obedience to authority, respect and hard-work, flung the door of elevation and prosperity open, and ushered her into the fulfillment of the promises of God concerning the redemption of mankind. Humility is always rewarded.

"Humble yourselves therefore under the mighty hand of God, that He may exalt you in due time" (I Peter 5:6). "Humble yourselves in the sight of the Lord, and He shall lift you up" (James 4:10).

Yes, her horn was exalted, when the marriage took place between her and Boaz. The process by which Boaz redeemed the inheritance of the dead and married Ruth was a symbol of our redemption. We were redeemed and betrothed to the Lord Jesus, our Redeemer. Ruth was redeemed and grafted into the lineage of the Messiah who was going to come to redeem mankind, because she was willing to leave her past behind, and walk into her future to become what God intended her to be right from creation.

OUR PAST CANNOT DICTATE OUR FUTURE

Ruth here represents us the Gentiles, whom God took and grafted into His chosen people so we could fulfill our destiny, and experienced salvation. Her faithfulness and self-sacrifice made her become a blessing to all the peoples of the world.

Daughters of the King, no matter how bad our past might have been, no matter how messed up you may be even now, there is still hope for the hopeless. God uses illegitimate and unwanted children for His glory. You may think you may not be effective in the hands of the Lord because of your background, but God can change our precedents into a beautiful picture of His grace and glory. If we can just get up from the old gutter, and take a bold step into the vast ocean of His amazing grace, He will ultimately change us, and use us to bless others.

The King, our heavenly Father, is still providing beauty in exchange for the ashes of our past. Please, do not dwell on your past, and never allow the enemy to beat you up with your past. There is always sunshine after the rain. Restoration is here! You never know what God can use someone for. If He spoke through Balaam's donkey, He can use anything. The Apostle Paul wrote:

> "For ye see your calling, brethren, how that not many wise men after the flesh, not many mighty, not many noble, are called: But God hath chosen the foolish things of the world to confound the wise; and God hath chosen the weak things of the world to confound the things which are mighty: And base things of the world, and things which are despised, hath God chosen, yea, and things which are not, to bring to naught things that are: That no flesh should glory in His presence. But of him are ye in Christ Jesus, who of God is made unto us wisdom, and righteousness, and sanctification, and redemption: That, according as it is written, He that glorieth, let him glory in the Lord" (I Corinthians 1:26-31).

My past wasn't pleasant. It was filled with idolatry, superstitions, a false religious spirit, untimely deaths, betrayals, pain, sicknesses, rejection and all kinds of unpleasant issues. Yet when I handed it all over to the Lord, He broke all those curses, healed, and is still healing, and molding me into the woman of God He designed me to be, right from the foundation of the earth. I am now willing and ready for Him to make me the vessel He desires me to be.

One day, as I began thinking about where He took me from, how He has kept me and where He is taking me, this song came into my spirit.

> There is sunshine after the rain
> There is sunshine after the rain
> It may rain, rain to flood your way
> It may rain, rain your dreams to take
> But the Spirit of the Lord
> A standard will raise
> To bring restoration
>
> There is healing after the pain
> There is glory after the shame
> It may quake, quake your faith to shake
> It may shake, shake your hope to break
> But the Spirit of the Lord
> A standard will raise
> To bring restoration
>
> Restoration is here, Yes, healing is here
> Won't you please take His hand?
> He is able to deliver and to set you free
> He's the Lifter of our heads

QUOTABLE QUOTES

"Is God all wise? Then the darkest providence has meaning. We will set ourselves as God's interpreters, and because we cannot make straight lines out of our crooked lot, we think that God has turned our lives into inextricable confusion. The darkest hours in our life have some intent, and it is really not needful that we should know all at once what that intent is. Let us keep within our own sphere, and live a day at a time, and breathe a breath at a time, and be content with one pulsation at a time, and interpretation will come when God pleases, and as He please."

Joseph Parker (1830-1902)

[5]

THE PROBLEM

(God Can Do All Things!)

❖

"What has been will be again, what has been done will be done again; there is nothing new under the sun. Is there anything of which one can say 'Look! This is new under the sun'? It was here already, long ago; it was here before our time" (Ecclesiastes 1:9-10).

I know that everything God does will endure forever; nothing can be added to it and nothing taken from it. God does it so that men will revere Him. Whatever is has already been, and what will be has been before; and God will call the past to account" (Ecclesiastes 3:14-15).

As the Holy Spirit took me through the book of Ruth, showing me these spiritual truths, I began to ask the Lord the reason why He is unveiling all these things to me. During one of these times, as I was digging into the heavenly manna – the Word – He was feeding me with, He said,

> "Monica, just as I prepared Ruth and other women for the coming of My Son into this world, so am I preparing feverishly many women for this last day revival, which will usher in the coming of My son to take His Bride home. ..."

The Holy Spirit had already spoken to me regarding the young people He is raising up to defy the enemy. So in continuing our conversation, I asked the Lord why He wants to use women also for this end-time revival. I wanted understand what part Ruth had in connection with this end-time anointing. The Lord spoke to my heart and said that the reason He took me through the book of Ruth was the fact that Ruth was a type of us the end-time daughters of the King that the Holy Spirit is wooing and calling unto Himself for this end-time revival.

You see the Church is a fusion of Gentiles and Jews – Ruth a Gentile marrying Boaz from the tribe of Judah. And Mary, the earthly mother of Christ our Lord represents the Messianic Jews. Today, the Church of Jesus Christ is the fusion of both Gentile Christians and Messianic Jews in Christ. Wow!

Ruth's gleaning at the time of the harvest is the message the Holy Spirit is sending to His end-time daughters to prepare themselves for a greater anointing and manifestations of the power of the Holy Spirit on all flesh, especially women. Many women are going to work side by side with men to harvest and glean the fields, making provision for the gifts and the fruit of the Holy Spirit to be operable in all dimensions.

As we see the day approaching, thus the anointing the Lord is going to pour out on many women is going to increase tremendously. There is a mighty outpouring of great anointing already coming upon all classes, all races, and colors of women world wide to ignite revival. The Holy Spirit is calling up a mighty army of women for this great move of God. This message was given to me when He spoke to me about sending me to the nations with His heart in 1992. The Lord spoke to me and said,

> "A time is coming and even at the door, when many women shall put on the mantle of leadership with great anointing; and the lies the enemy planted into their lives shall be dismantled in My name ...... Prepare yourself for it. ....."

Having a little doubt about myself, and the lies society has been telling women today especially in the third world, I could not believe the message was from the Lord. Having ministered in Africa and specifically the country in which I ministered side by side with my husband, women are not even ordained for ministry, let alone sharing the same anointing. Their entitlement was just to be quiet and obedient to their husbands, to work within their perimeter; that is to minister to women, and not to men.

In view of this good news the Lord gave me, I asked Him again and again as I fasted and prayed, *'Lord, why women also for this end-time revival?'* The Lord's reply really stunned me. Here is what He said,

> "In the beginning when man (Adam and Eve) was created, I gave man authority and dominion over everything and made him the overseer of all things

that I created, but to the woman, it was different. Adam was the protector and the preserver of all My creation. While Adam was sleeping as I fashioned the woman, I kept My secret with the woman as I communed with her spirit. There is something peculiar about women that are not in men. I planted My seed in the woman and made her a prophetic blessing in disguise to the whole world. I deposited in the woman the ability to reproduce. I gave her the grace to bear pain as well as utilizing her pain to bring life to many. I gave the woman the secret of My heart — of passion and compassion, of tenderness toward her offspring, of love unfeigned for humanity. I implanted into her a servant heart to serve all without wavering, and gave her an enduring heart .... Hence the reason the enemy also tempted Eve first and not Adam. ... I knew that through her Seed, the head of the enemy shall be crushed, ushering in My Kingdom forever after the fall of satan—a Kingdom without sin, an everlasting Kingdom. This is the reason I identify Myself many times with the woman in My dealings with mankind. ..."

Do you see why the enemy tempted Eve, the mother of all humanity?
From the day Eve yielded to the lies of the enemy, she lost the heart of God. The woman's passion for God was reduced. Everything God implanted into her was abridged to nothing, because she handed over her God-given privileges and authority to the enemy – satan. The false step she took affected the whole human race. Her godly passion turned into lust. She was turned loose to every evil desire to satisfy her flesh. Her compassion turned into hatred for her own offspring, deliberately killing her unborn, and neglecting her children. All satan instigated.

Today some women do not want to have children, because they cannot stand the pain of taking care of someone else. A lot of women have turned to alcohol, drugs, prostitution, witchcraft, and every evil deed of the flesh (I kings 3:16-27). Yes, the enemy has taken the God-given sympathy and empathy away from them. In the book of II Kings 6:25-29, we see an example of women eating up their own children to satisfy their hunger.

She lost her ability to feel pain for her young ones. Apparently, many women have become anesthetized and insensible. They do not care for anyone; not even for their young ones. Isn't it ridiculous? Yes, some women are now capable of abandoning and even killing their own children to satisfy their sensual evil desires. Women gained the ability to lie and to be lied to, cheat and be cheated, deceive and be deceived et cetera.

Yes, she lost her God-consciousness and gained self-consciousness. All that most women started thinking of, and still are, is self-beauty, self appreciation, self satisfaction, and spending their wealth to satisfy the self's craving. The book of Proverbs makes it clear that outward beauty is vain without the fear of the Lord.

> "Many daughters have done virtually, but thou excellest them all. Favor is deceitful, and beauty is vain, but a woman that fearest the Lord, she shall be praised. Give her of the fruit of her hands; and let her own works praise her in the gates" (Proverbs 31:29-31).

The beauty that God requires is that of a quiet, gentle and a humble spirit, which reflects the character and beauty of Christ.

"Whose adorning let it not be that outward adorning of plaiting the hair, and of wearing of gold, or of putting on of apparel; but let it be the hidden man of the heart, in that which is not corruptible, even the ornament of a meek and quiet spirit, which is in the sight of God of great price" (I Peter 3:2-5).

* * * * * * *

The woman also lost the spirit of servant-hood to care and serve her Lord, her husband and her family, abandoning her family life and racing for 'impressive' things. (Please read Proverbs 31:10-31).

From the moment of the fall, satan has been trying to destroy womankind through her choices in believing a lie and disobeying God's command. Why? Satan was present when we were created. Satan saw what the Father endowed humanity with, especially the woman. Once satan lost his heavenly privileges, he became jealous of us. It was through his own rebellion and pride that he lost his position in heaven. Read Isaiah 14:12-15; Ezekiel 28:1-19.

As you know, Lucifer was the chief choirmaster in heaven. He enjoyed the glorious presence of the Almighty. He had authority over the angelic choristers under his control (Isaiah 14:12-16). But his own arrogance and pride had brought him down. Now he is devastated because he cannot even repent to be restored. He is angry because man is the only creature among God's creation, which is created in the image of the Almighty, and is redeemable. Yes, and the secret God endowed the woman with was being coveted by the adversary. Hence the reason he used every means to separate the woman from her Creator.

When the Lord's verdict came upon the human race, including the serpent, there was a promise given which we have to fully comprehend.

"I will put enmity between you and the woman, that between your offspring and hers, he will crush your head, and you will strike his heels" (Gen 3:15).

Every Bible scholar knows this promise was about the coming of our Lord and Savior Jesus Christ to crush the head of the serpent. But it also embodied the restoration of the woman into her former state of knowing her Creator more than ever; to move in that direction to counteract the work of the enemy. The promise in Genesis 3:15, was very profound. In other words, the Lord was saying,

"Satan, there will be a long struggle between good and evil, bad choices and good decisions as you would strike man's heels to keep him down, but My purpose will surely stand! Just as you used this woman to doubt My heart in order to destroy My plan for humanity, I will use this same woman's Seed (Jesus, My Son) to crush your head and destroy your kingdom. A time will come when your venom shall be removed, your stings shall be destroyed, at what time My redemptive work for mankind shall be paid in full; when restoration shall bring out all My secrets out of the very vessel you used to disrupt My plan and purposes. Then will come a great anointing upon women to counteract your evil plan and deception, and to bring about a revival for Mine own glory."

As I began jotting down what He was telling me, I heard in my heart these words, *"In the beginning, the enemy used the woman to interrupt My plan. At the close of this age, I am going to turn it all round and use the same 'woman' to destroy the kingdom of the enemy, and promote the kingdom of God."* Hallelujah! What a glorious end women are going to have!

BIBLICAL TORCHBEARERS AND IGNITERS

From the moment of the fall, the Lord began a journey, searching to find His heart in any woman who would make herself available. Starting from the Old Testament, the Spirit of the Lord found few women whose hearts were bent on finding God's will and purposes for their lives. As these women began to emerge, the Lord also began to weave and interweave His plan and purposes in order to bring about His redemptive work for mankind, starting from a woman's consecration. A few examples of these women will give you a glimpse of what the Spirit is trying to convey to us, the end-time daughters of the King.

Rebecca – She became the "wife of an oath." Abraham obligated his servant to swear that he would not go contrary to the word given in choosing a wife for his son among his brethren. And before the servant ever finished praying, God answered his prayer, and Rebecca became Isaac's wife (Genesis 24). When she became pregnant with the twins, she received a word from the Lord. *"Two nations are in your womb, and two peoples from within you will be separate; one people will be stronger than the other, and the older shall serve the younger" (Genesis 25 21-23).* Rebecca was given a glimpse into the realm of the spirit, of what the younger son was going to be—a mighty nation through whom the Redeemer would come to redeem humanity. Against all odds, she chose to bring Jacob into the blessings designed for him before he was ever conceived. Her act of faith ushered Jacob into his destiny. Through Jacob, came the nation of Israel, and through Judah of Jacob, the Messiah emerged. Rebecca was a visionary.

Jochebed – She was the mother of Moses. She was a woman of faith who had compassion and consideration for her baby boy. Having an eye of faith, she knew her son was not an ordinary child. She knew that child had a destiny and fought for his survival. God honored her faith, and she became the caretaker of her own child. Jochebed imbedded the knowledge of the true God into Moses' little life, as she weaned him for a pagan princess. Moses became the deliverer of Israel from Pharaoh's bondage. Jochebed was anointed to preserve life (Exodus 2:1-3, 8-9; Hebrews 11:23).

Miriam – She was the sister of Moses. She was a woman of passion who became the watchwoman of her brother. Courageous and caring, she was able to approach the Egyptian princess, and through her counsel, Moses' own mother nursed her baby and inculcated in him the fear of Jehovah God. Obviously, Miriam's passion for the salvation of others drew her closer to become the spokeswoman of God, a prophetess. Her zeal for God spontaneously drove her in praise and worship to the Lord God Jehovah, who had wrought great signs and wonders to deliver His people from bondage (Exodus 2: 4-7; Exodus 15:1-21).

Deborah – She was a common woman just like all of us, for the Bible spoke clearly of her as a wife, a mother, a judge and a prophetess. She had a handful of things to accomplish every day as a mother and a wife. Yet she made herself available to bring the people of God into a right relationship with the Lord as a judge, and through her counsel, men and women rose up to fulfill their God given destiny. Through her encouragement as a mentor to all Israel, their enemies were destroyed. Deborah had the heart of God (Judges 4, 5).

Jael – She was an ordinary wife and mother, through whose gentleness, and hospitality, the enemy entered her tent. By her generosity, her enemy slept at her feet, and as a warrior, she courageously crushed the head of the foe, and Israel had peace. Jael was a type of an end-time warrior (Judges 4:17-24, 5:24-27).

Ruth – By her marriage to Judah's offspring, she signed a contract with the Lion of the tribe of Judah. By her declaration, *"Your God shall be my God..."* she forsook all and made herself a sacrifice worthy of praise and honor. By her dedication and submission to Naomi, she became a candidate for royalty. Her gleaning in the harvest portrayed her desire to be whatever God designed her to be without complaint. Her gleaning in the field during harvest, together with the men and women, was a type of this end-time revival and great anointing going to be poured on all flesh before the coming of the Lord. Hence she received the anointing to become an instrument of blessing to all humanity. For God found in her His heart, and so it was through her seed that King David emerged and our dear Lord and Savior was born to redeem us from our sins.

Abigail – What a beauty of character! She was beautiful inside and outside! Through her calm and gentle attitude, David's anger was appeased. Through her generosity and quiet spirit, she became God's instrument of peace that preserved David from shedding blood. God avenged David of his enemies in His own time. Abigail fought not with carnal weapons of mass destruction, but with a quiet and a gentle spirit, filled with grace and servant-hood – A type of God's ordinary, yet extraordinary vessels, who are surfacing with grace and gentleness in bringing salvation to the unloved. Read 1Samuel chapter 25.

Mary – She was the mother of our Lord. A humble, God-fearing young woman, whose story has been told countless times. At the time she came into view, God's woven instrument of redemption caught her heart. She had already made herself ready to be the candidate for the fulfillment of God's promise of sending the Seed. By her choosing to live a holy life, the Holy God could spin His thread through her heart to communicate His desires to her. By being a virgin, she fit into God's requirement and plan for Him to lay His bed in her womb, so she could bring forth the Holy Seed without contamination of the original sin; because it would take holiness and righteousness to eliminate the curse of sin upon humanity. The Holy Spirit designed Mary for that purpose. By her submission to the will of God in bearing the Seed, Mary became an asset through which God would now usher women into the new move of God to carry the seed of the end-time revival until the end of this age.

Anna – She was one time a young woman who married for only seven years. At a young age her husband died. Anna decided to consecrate the rest of her life to wait upon the Lord in prayers and fasting, night and day in the temple, waiting for the coming of the Messiah. The instant she saw the baby Jesus, she knew He was the Redeemer of mankind. Her dream was fulfilled. Anna was a prophetess who knew the heart of God (Luke 2:36-38).

Praise the Lord! At God's appointed time, the Seed came. Restoration began to take its course step by step.

- Women sat at His feet to listen to the 'Word become flesh' (John 1:1-3; Luke 10:38-42).
- Women provided for His needs (Luke 8:1-3).
- Women followed Him everywhere He went and received their dead raised, their health restored, and demons cast out (Luke 7:11-16, 8:43-48, 13:11-17).
- Women showed gratitude by washing His feet with their tears. Mary unsoiled His feet with her hair and anointed Him (Luke 7:36-40).
- Women passionately followed Him weeping and wailing when He was condemned to die, and when

Jesus gave the prophecy of Jerusalem's desolation (Luke 23:26-31).
- Women followed Him avidly and stood beneath the Cross without fear or looking back when all the disciples fled with the exception of John (John 19:25-27; Mark 15:40-41).
- Women went fearlessly to the tomb to anoint His body, regardless of the fact that the sepulcher had been sealed and soldiers guarded it (Matthew 27:62-66, Luke 23:55-56; 24:1).
- Women were the first to witness the triumph of Christ over Satan, death, hell and the grave (Mark 16:1-6, Luke 24:1-12).
- Women were the first to receive the commission to go and tell the good news of His resurrection, even to the disciples (Matthew 28:5-8, Mark 16: 6-8).
- Women received the baptism of the Holy Spirit, and were endowed with power as they tarried with all the apostles in the upper room (Acts 1:8-14, Acts 2:1-4, 16-21).

What more shall we say about Priscilla, about Lydia, about Dorcas, Phoebe, and many others in the New Testament? All these women were just a foretaste of what the Holy Spirit was planning for this end-time before the coming of our Lord and Savior.

These few examples are biblical facts about God's dealings with women pointing to the next move of the Holy Spirit upon women who will make themselves available.

19th CENTURY FORERUNNERS

As the years after the apostles passed by, the Holy Spirit did not leave a witness of His call upon women. He began raising up women one at a time to stir up revivals during the

Dark Ages and in the beginning of the revivals in the 17th and the 18th centuries. These women became great evangelists, teachers, mentors, writers, songwriters and so forth.

In the 1900's came women such as Corrie Ten Boom and Kathryn Kulhmann. These two women became my inspiration while I prayed every day asking the Lord to make me like them. I have not been in a concentration camp like Corrie ten Boom, but my prayer was partially answered as I have suffered a lot for the name of Christ. I have not yet attained the level of anointing Kathryn Kulhmann had, but I am praying and seeking the face of the Lord to make me a part of this end-time army of women He is raising up for His own glory.

Corrie ten Boom and her sister Betsie, became the object of scorn, suffering, and imprisonment in Nazi prison for hiding Jews in their homes. Although Betsie entered glory prematurely through human atrocities in prison, she walked into the arms of her Jewish Messiah, whose cause she had defended faithfully, and whose words she had kept and suffered for. (Matthew 25:31-40). Even though Corrie was later on released from prison, she literally bore on her heart the memory of the atrocities she saw in prison. Her faith and courage is known all around the world, because she chose to be a bridge of hospitality, of protection, an anchor of hope to God's people, an igniter of true faith in Christ, and good works towards others.

Sabrina Wumbrand and her husband suffered terribly in prison for spreading the gospel. Her unbending faith and courage in face of suffering for the cause of Christ; her zeal in spreading the Word, and loving her torturers is worthy of emulation. Through her and her husband, we have now a voice (Voice of the Martyr), all around the world, praying and advocating for the persecuted of the Christian faith.

Lillian Trasher, a woman of passion, whose acts of compassion shall never be forgotten by the Egyptians. She pioneered an orphanage in Egypt, which has produced today men and women of caliber—some in ministry, some in government leadership, and others still being used by the Master in different fields for His glory.

In 1944, Gladys Hinson founded the children's home in Arkansas now named Hillcrest. It is located in the rolling Ouachita hills and mountains, surrounding Hot Springs, Arkansas. With 10 cents in her purse and a call to missions, Gladys birthed this vision that has blessed thousands of children and still is. She is gone, but her work remains.

Mother Teresa's acts of compassion in Calcutta (India), is widely praised by the world. Walking down the streets and ministering to dying and hungry souls, became the norm for her. She literally brought life and hope to dying, hungry, and rejected children of India. She will forever be remembered.

For the past five to twenty years, we have seen an innumerable army of women the Holy Spirit has raised for His glory. Let us take just a little look at our surroundings to mention just a few, such as: Marilyn Hickey and Sarah, Joyce Meyers, Stormie Omartian, Liberty Savard, Beth Moore, Judy Jacobs, Karen Wheaton, Paula White, Gloria Copeland, Juanita Bynum, Pat Chen and other women of God. These women are just a foretaste of what the Holy Spirit is about to do if we get up from the dust of our past, and allow Him to clean us up and be used for His own glory.

Now, what else should convince all "women haters" of the fact of God's end-time anointing upon women? The mighty wall of human ideologies and religion, erected against women, is being crumbled by the Holy Spirit, because God is raising up for Himself a mighty army of women from all around the world. They are living brands plugged out of the fires. The cultural and religious prejudices that hindered the call of God as it pertains to women are being removed. It is coming, slowly but surely because the mouth of the Lord has spoken it.

For example, in the fulfillment of prophecy in the Bible, God used a Gentile woman, Ruth to become the breaker of the wall of separation (erected to hinder God's pre-ordained purposes for humanity), thereby pre-fulfilling Apostle Paul's revelation of no distinction in Christ. He wrote,

"There is neither Jew nor Greek, there is neither bond nor free, there is neither male nor female: for ye are all one in Christ" (Galatians 3:28).

The King's daughters have been restored because of Christ, and any woman can be a candidate for this end-time anointing but there is a price to pay. I am grateful to the Lord because I am a part of a church that believes in the ministry of women. However, sisters, remember: *"God did not choose us because we were worthy, but by choosing us He makes us worthy"* says Thomas Watson (1557-1592).

The other reason is the fact that many men have vacated their God-given role of being the head of the home, and the priest of the family. Rampant divorces and infidelities, internet pornography, pride, and arrogance have taken hold of many men, including even some ministers. The gear is being shifted from men to women. Ladies prepare, the tide is rising very fast, catch the waves and soar higher or be left behind! However, beware! The greater the anointing, the faster and quicker judgment falls!

QUOTABLE QUOTES

"God loves you dearly. He is willing to discipline you in order that you may share in His holiness and enjoy the blessings He has in store for the obedient Christian... The rod of God keeps you in His safe pasture and protects you from the consequences of foolish decisions."

Charles Stanley (1932-)

[6]

END-TIME VESSELS

(Vessels Who Are Willing To Pay The Price!)

❖

"In a large house there are articles not only of gold and silver, but also of wood and clay; some are for noble purposes and some for ignoble. If a man cleanses himself (herself) from the latter, he (she) will be an instrument for noble purposes, made holy, useful to the Master and prepared to do any good work" (2 Timothy 2:20-21).

"If anyone would come after me, he must deny himself and take up his cross and follow me. For whosoever wants to save his life will lose it, but whoever loses his life for me and for the gospel will save it" (Mark 8:34-35).

The Word is being given, the horn is being sounded, but who are these end-time candidates for this revival?

A look at all the preceding revivals starting from the Acts of the Apostles to the early revivals in the past centuries, we get a clear picture of the price that was paid before these revivals became possible. They went through the fires of persecutions, of trials, rejections, and even martyrdom, yet they held on to the faith, proclaiming the Word of Lord with zeal and perseverance.

It is also important and imperative to know that the recipients of these end-time moves of God are not exempt from paying greater prices like our predecessors in order to be the kind of vessels that are sold out for God. These end-time daughters of the King are vessels that have living stories to tell the world. They have known the faithfulness of their Heavenly Father and have learned submission and obedience through the things they have suffered and are ready to launch out into the deep with the Lord of the harvest.

As I communed with the Lord, This is what He told me. "The vessels I am preparing are women who are willing to pay the price in every aspect of their lives." Dr. T. D. Jakes, in one of his preaching, made a comment with reference to some preachers or Christians who desired a portion of the anointing that is upon his life. He made it clear that the anointing he has today is a direct result of the things he went through.

In other words, being used of God or having a mighty anointing upon one's life is not a cheap deal. Many of us have come to where we are today, because of what we have been through with the Lord.

QUOTABLE QUOTES

"There is no situation so chaotic that God cannot from that situation create something that is surpassingly good. He did it at creation. He did it at the cross. He is doing it today.

Bishop Handley Carr Glyn Moule (1841-1920)

[7]

WOMEN WHO HAVE BEEN THROUGH THE FIRES
(Refined And Purified For Service)

❖

"He is like a refiner's fire ... and He shall sit as a refiner and purifier of silver; and He shall purify the sons of Levi, and purge them as gold and silver, that they may offer unto the Lord an offering of righteousness" (Mal 3:2-3, RSV).

"...That the trials of your faith, being much more precious than of gold that perisheth, though it be tried with the fire, might be found unto praise and honor and glory at the appearing of Jesus Christ. Whom having not seen, ye love; in whom, though now ye see Him not, yet believing, ye rejoice with joy unspeakable and full of glory" (1 Peter 1:3-8 summarized).

God has come down many times on earth through fire to speak to His people, to judge them, to equip them, and also to instill Godly fear and reverence. He spoke to Moses through the fires of the unburnable bush, and anointed him for ministry (Exodus 3). He spoke to the children of Israel through the fire at Mt Horeb (Deuteronomy 4:10-14). He judged Nadab and Abihu with fire from heaven (Leviticus 10:1-3). Fire fell from heaven to consume the sacrifice of king Solomon, as his prayers of dedication touched the throne-room of God. At Mount Carmel, The Lord came down in fire to consume the sacrifice, the wood, the stones and the soil, and licked up the water in the trench (I Kings 18:16-39). John the Baptist, inspired by the Holy Ghost, declared,

"I baptize you with water for repentance. But after me will come one who is more powerful than I, whose sandals I am not fit to carry. He will baptized you with the Holy Spirit and with fire" (Matthew 3:11)

On the day of Pentecost, when the fire of the Holy Spirit came down, He consumed their bickering and complaining, their selfish ambitions, and empowered them for service (Acts 2). The Lord is taking His vessels through the fires to burn all the unholy alliances, all compromises, all fleshly evil tendencies in order to make us useful vessels in His hands.

Do you see what is happening today as you watch most of the Christian channels? Have you listened closely to their stories or testimonies to know where they are coming from and the reason they are on fire for the Lord? Praise the Lord! They are all coming out of a kind of fire. This is the reason they are angry with the enemy, not with human offenders. They have deep burning desire to be instruments of righteousness and hope to free others. Yes, they've been through the fire.

They have been through the fire, what does it mean? Fire has a whole lot of connotation, but we will only consider these three.

- **Fire speaks of Refining and Cleansing.**

"For Thou, O God, hast proved us: Thou hast tried us, as silver is tried. Thou broughtest us into the net; Thou laidest affliction upon our loins. Thou hast caused men to ride over our heads; we went through fire and through water: but Thou broughtest us out into a wealthy place" (Psalms 66:10-12).

Goldsmiths and silversmiths use fire to cleanse and refine their product. When gold is taken out of the mine, it is always dirty and covered with filth. In order for the owner or the smith to get the gold out of the filth, he washes it with water, and grinds away all the impurities. He then refines it with fire; then rebuffs it before fashioning it according to His purpose and designs. According to a few goldsmiths I have spoken to in Africa, they recognize or come to the conclusion the gold or silver is ready for use or sale when they see their reflections in their product.

God's ultimate purpose in refining us is to see the beauty of Christ reflecting in us. For the Holy Spirit to get the deposited treasure out of our lives, we must go through His cleansing and His refinery. He washes us first with water, which is the acceptance of Christ as Savior through faith in the Word of God. He proceeds the second time with His fire to take away the dross. Then He rebuffs us with the power of His Spirit to equip us to be able ministers of His Kingdom. This is a wonderful process but not easy.

- **Fire supernaturally also expresses God's nature of holiness, and of vengeance**

    "Wherefore we receiving a kingdom which cannot be moved, let us have grace, whereby we may serve God acceptably with reverence and godly fear: For our God is a consuming fire" (Hebrews 12:28-29).

    Our God is holy and demands holiness from His children. In his book, "The Fire of His Holiness," our beloved brother and Pastor Sergio Scataglini's passion for God was demonstrated in the way he wrote concerning the holiness of God. His account of what the Lord told him sparked an innate desire to be 100% holy, pure and clean from all sin. The Lord told him:

    "I wish you could be as cold as a pagan, so I could save you again, or as hot as a believer that has given 100% to Me. Then I could use you in My own way. Because you are neither hot nor cold, I will spit you out of My mouth. 98% holiness is not enough." (End of quote)

    You see, 98% holiness is not enough for God! It is imperative we ponder about this.

    When you read the book of Isaiah chapter six, we get the clear picture of cleansing before and during service. The prophet Isaiah had been on his prophetic job for some time. Yet it was during the time of king Uzziah's death that he had an encounter with the holiness of the Lord. As he stood before the throne of God in awe of His holiness, he saw his own wretchedness. But when he had cried out about his woes, an angel of God took a live coal (fire) from the altar and cleansed his lips. It was after he was cleansed that Isaiah received a fresh revelation to respond fully to the call of

God; and was re-commissioned afresh with fresh anointing to the nations (both Israel and the surrounding nations), with a message that has transformed lives and kingdoms.

> "In the year that king Uzziah died, I saw the Lord seated on a throne, high and exalted.... And they were calling to one another: "Holy, holy, holy is the Lord Almighty; the whole earth is filled with His glory." ...'Woe to me!' I cried, "I am ruined! For I am a man of unclean lips, and I live among a people of unclean lips, and my eyes have seen the King, the Lord Almighty." Then one of the seraphs flew to me with a live coal in his hand, which he had taken with tongs from the altar. With it he touched my mouth and said, "See, this has touched your lips; your guilt is taken away and your sin atoned for." Then I heard the voice of the Lord saying, "Whom shall I send? And who will go for us?" And I said, "Here am I, send me!" (Isaiah 6:1-8, NIV).

The Lord our God is also a God of vengeance, but we are not a people under His wrath. We've been saved from the wrath to come through the shed blood of Christ (Romans 5:9; 1 Thessalonians 5:9). The Prophet Isaiah said,

> "Who among us can dwell with the devouring fire? Who among us can dwell with the everlasting burnings? He who walks righteously and speaks uprightly, who despises the gain of oppressions, who shakes his hands, lest they hold a bribe, who stops his ears from hearing of bloodshed and shuts his eyes from looking upon evil..." (Isaiah 33:14-15, RSV).

The writer of the book of Hebrews also affirms this fact with an admonition to heed the voice of God. *"Wherefore we receiving a kingdom which cannot be moved, let us have grace whereby we may serve God acceptably with reverence and godly fear: For our God is a consuming fire" (Hebrews 12:28-29, KJV).*

- **Fire also seals a covenant. (Genesis 15:17-18)**

"When the sun had set and darkness had fallen, a smoking firepot with a blazing torch appeared and passed between the pieces. On that day, the Lord made a covenant with Abram and said, "To your descendants I give this land, from the river of Egypt to the great river, Euphrates ..." (Genesis 15:17-18 NIV).

In Genesis chapter 15:17-18, we see the Lord Jehovah making a covenant with Abraham. Abraham had already left his family as commanded by the Lord. The Lord had blessed him because of his obedience, but there was conflict between him and his nephew Lot because of their possessions. Lot selfishly chose the land that was greener and flourishing and left Abraham on the desert part. Yet Abraham's unselfishness led him to rescue Lot and his family from the hand of their enemies, when the kings of the land had a battle and Lot's family was captured.

Coming from his conquest, Abraham met Melchizedek and gave him the tithes of all the goods. Melchizedek, a type of Christ, gave his blessings to Abraham in return. Abraham also refused to have any part with the king of Sodom. (This is a different message in itself). It was subsequent to all these exploits that the Lord renewed His promises to him and asked for an offering. After Abraham had followed the instructions given to him, the Lord came down in the form of a smoking furnace and a burning lamp and passed through the offering, and that same day He made a covenant with Abraham.

* * * * * * *

These end-time vessels that the Lord is preparing must go through the fire for cleansing and purification. As said earlier, the Holy Spirit must get His deposited treasure out of us in order for Him to use us effectively.

"....If a man cleanses himself from the latter, he will be an instrument for noble purposes, made holy, useful to the master and prepared to do any good work" (II Timothy 2:21 NIV).

How will He do that? By taking each vessel through the fire! Many have already gone through this fire, others are going through it, and there are some yet to go through. This fire can be anything, which He may use to make us what He intends to use us for. There are fires of sickness and diseases. There are fires of trials, persecutions, betrayal, and insecurities. There are fires of loss of loved ones, bereavement, and grief. There are also fires of divorce and being single or/ and loneliness. Yes, fires, fires, and fires; fires to refine, and single you out for a great testimony of Who He Is.

Do you know that Ruth also went through the fire? Her past family history was fire in itself. Then she went through the fire of seeing her loved one dying, the harshness of widowhood and its accompanied solitude.

LIFE SPRINGS OUT OF DEATH

The Lord had been telling my husband and me since 1995 to leave Togo (West Africa) for the United States. We were pastors of a mega church with thousands of members. Moreover, we had everything we needed and did not need anything from the United States. We did not want to do that. He dealt with us over and over through Word of knowledge and prophecies from even strangers, but we continued to postpone our obedience, and somehow despised all the warnings.

Finally, He started dealing with me particularly and reminding me of what He had told me years before, even before I married. He kept on telling me I am a vessel called to the nations. I thought I had nothing to offer to anyone, and so I could not even convince my husband to leave until disaster struck. We went through an unbelievable betrayal and trials I have never dreamt of. After all the painful, demonic orchestrated lies, my husband passed away, broken hearted.

In my dilemma, I thought it was all over for me. While Geoffrey was dying, he kept on telling me to obey the Lord and not stay in Togo; yet I still felt my world was over. Until some few days after the funeral, the Lord gave me another chance of leaving Togo for the United States. He said this to me when I finally decided to obey fully,

> "Monica, life always springs out of death. My Son died so that the world might have life. Geoffrey's death is the beginning of your ministry in a different dimension. I am not finished with you yet. This is just the beginning of what I can use you to accomplish for My glory. I am sending you to the nations with My heart to touch children, young people, women and all classes of people for My Name sake and for My glory.........." (Summary)

He even told me it was because of me the borders of the United States had not been tightened up, and that it would soon be tough for people to enter the States. This warning was very frightening and I had to obey. I have been in the United States since December 2001. Since I obeyed, I have seen the Lord begin to use me in many ways I thought impossible, and I believe there is more yet to come for His glory. All these trials have a purpose.

> "… The genuineness of your faith, being much precious than gold that perishes, though it is tested by fire, may be found to praise, honor, and glory at the revelation of Jesus Christ, whom having not seen you love" (I Peter I: 6-8).

The Master did not promise us 'bread and butter' all the time. Neither did He say honey would drip on our tongues every second of our walk with Him. He rather recommended that we should deny ourselves and to take up our crosses and follow Him.

> "And when He had called the people unto Him with His disciples also, He said unto them, 'Whosoever will come after Me, let him deny himself, and take up his cross, and follow Me" (Mark 8:34).

Sisters, the cross depicts or represents shame, rejection, suffering, persecutions, pain, and all kinds of difficult situations any child of God can go through for the sake of Christ. Almost all the apostles suffered persecutions, imprisonment and martyrdom.

The apostle Peter knew what going through the fire looks like. His own past failures and mistakes, his zeal and misconduct when the Master was arrested, and his denial of the Lord Jesus three times, was just a glimpse of what he was being prepared to go through as a faithful servant of the Lord. He then faced many imprisonments and scourging after Pentecost when the lame man walked miraculously in the Name above all names. In spite of all these, he writes to us in simple admonition a propos to the great inheritance we have in Christ Jesus that can never perish, spoil or fade away.

"……. Though now for a little while you may have had to suffer grief in all kinds of trials. These have come so that your faith – of greater worth than gold, which perishes even though refined by fire – may be proved genuine and may result in praise, glory and honor when Jesus Christ is revealed" (I Peter 1:6-7 NIV).

So the Apostle Peter gives us two reasons why we go through the fire. First: That we may be proved genuine – saturated with unbendable faith in Christ and His finished work. Second: That the result of all these fires may bring glory, praise and honor to the Lord.

In view of these two reasons given by the apostle Peter, our brother James picks it up and encourages us to take it calmly, and rejoice when we go through the fires. Adding to that of the apostle Peter, James gives us a few reasons why we can go through the fire with confidence.

"Consider it pure joy, my brothers, whenever you face trials of many kinds, because you know that the testing of your faith develops perseverance. Perseverance must finish its work so that you may be mature and complete, not lacking anything.... Blessed is the man who perseveres under trial, because when he has stood the test, he will receive the crown of life, which God has promised to those who love Him" (James 1:2-4, 12).

However, he marks out clearly that without the fire, we can never develop perseverance. We need perseverance in soul winning. We need perseverance in prayer like Elijah in order to receive the answers to our prayers. We need perseverance in our walk with the Lord in order to prove to the critics of our faith in Christ that our Lord is faithful. We need perseverance in everything. Yet it takes testing and trials to build this characteristic in us. Brother James enumerates two examples of trials (fires) of great men that resulted in great blessings — The Prophets of old and Job.

Although these prophets of old suffered atrociously, they persistently labored and walked with the Lord. Some were put into dungeons and fed with water and bread. Some were killed between or on the altars of God. Some were put into fiery furnaces, others were stoned, yet they declared to their persecutors that they believed their God would deliver them; and even if He doesn't, they would not bow to their images. The fires turned out to be supernatural air-conditioners because the fourth person showed up. Some had their beds in-between lions. Some were beheaded. Some were imprisoned, but they turned their prison into a musical concert in singing praises to their Lord. These are the heroes the book of Hebrews talks about.

> "And what more shall I say? I do not have time to talk about Gideon, Barak, Samson, Jephthah, David, Samuel and the prophets, who through faith conquered kingdoms, administered justice, and gained what was promised; who shut the mouth of lions, quenched the fury of the flames, and escaped the edge of the sword; whose weakness was turned to strength; and who became powerful in battle and routed foreign enemies. Women received back their dead, raised to life again. Others were tortured and refused to be released, so that they might gain a better resurrection. Some faced jeers and flogging, while still others were chained and put into prison. They were stoned; they were sawed in two; they were put

to death by the sword. They went about in sheepskins and goatskins, destitute, persecuted and mistreated – the world was not worthy of them. They wandered in deserts and mountain, and in caves and holes in the ground" (Heb 11:32-38 NIV).

In their fires of pain, persecutions, afflictions and all that these heroes suffered, I have come to the conclusion that they went through all that they did because the Lord was their passion. They fought the good fight. They finished their courses faithfully for the reason that there was a mighty driving force within them – their love, their passion and their unfeigned faith in the One who called them out of darkness into His marvelous light.

The apostle's reference to Job's sufferings is very familiar to Christians and non-Christians alike, but he makes a comment on how Job's perseverance in the fire brought about great blessings to him afterwards.

> "As you know, we consider blessed those who have persevered. You have heard of Job's perseverance and have seen what the Lord finally brought about. The Lord is full of compassion and mercy" (James 5:11).

We all know that the enemy orchestrated whatever Job went through; yet, it was God's stamp of approval on Job's life of integrity. God openly boasted that His servant Job was faithful, and challenged Satan that Job would not curse Him even in times of great trial. He therefore gave the adversary, and the accuser of the brethren, permission to take His servant Job through the fires. In one day, Job lost everything—his children and his property.

Was it easy for Job when the Lord gave permission to the enemy? No! No and No! Job did not have a clue of what was happening. In his desperation through the fires of loss, affliction, and persecution from even his own friends, he sought to find the hand of God in whatever was happening, but God was silent. His own wife asked him to curse God and die, as we all know. As for Job, I could see tears in his eyes and head down, crying out in anguish saying,

> "But if I go to the east, He is not there; if I go to the west, I do not find Him. When He is at work in the north, I do not see Him; when He turns to the south, I catch no glimpse of Him" (Job 23:8-9 NIV).

In other words, Job is saying, "Lord, where are You in all these? I do not feel Your presence, and You have left me to my own demise. Please, I need to hear from You."

On the other hand, did Job ever know he was going to be restored in the future, and even more than what he lost? I hope not. Yet in the last phase of the fires burning on his skin, he could say, *"But He knows the way that I take; when He has tested me, I will come forth as gold"* (Job 23:10 NIV).

Yes, Job came forth like gold from the fire and became a high priest to his 'ignorant' friends, and a blessing to others, because he was restored through perseverance and the knowledge of God's sovereignty (Job 38—42).

PERSONAL EXPERIENCE

It is excruciatingly heart breaking when God is silent at the time you need Him most. I become sometimes overwhelmed, frustrated, and inundated with the weight of my problem; however, there is a purpose or a reason when God is silent. During this time, be assured, He is working out everything for your good at His own appointed time.

"I will stand on my watch and station myself on the rampart; I will look to see what He will say to me, and what answer I am to give to this complaint. Then the Lord replied: "Write down the revelation and make it plain on tablets so that a herald may rush with it. For the revelation awaits an appointed time; it speaks of the end and will not prove false. Though it lingers, wait for it. It will certainly come and will not delay" (Habakkuk 2:1-3).

My own testimony proves this fact. I have asked Him many times why He took Geoffrey away. For three months He did not speak until one afternoon, after I had cried my eyes out in the room alone, screaming, *"Lord, please, why? Please, please speak. I am ready to listen and to comply with Your decision."* That day I was taken aback with what He said to me.

First of all, He said, "I had My secret with Geoffrey. He never shared that with you. It was not cancer that killed My servant, and Geoffrey knew that. Cancer was just a channel through which My servant came home."

Secondly, "When I have told you all that you need to know about My will and you don't follow My instructions, the only thing I can do is to make you willing to obey." Yes, we learn obedience through the things that come our way; especially when it is orchestrated by the Lord.

Thirdly, "I do not compete with anyone; neither do I share My chosen vessel with anybody. Whatever you cherish more than Me, shall be taken away so I can get your attention. I am a jealous God." The Lord is always right! I know that perfectly well.

MATURITY IS A PROCESS

In continuing with James' exhortation, he encourages us that it takes perseverance to make one mature, complete and lacking nothing.

"... but let patience have its perfect work, that you may be perfect, and complete, lacking nothing" (James 1:4).

James' analogy in the passage we read can be compared to human growth. Children that were protected and sheltered; carried often, and pampered, remain babies, even when grown. They have no sense of maturity. They have not developed strong bones, and they do not know how to make decisions for themselves. Although now adult physically, they are always depending on others to guide them. They are always depending on others to provide for their needs. They can't help anybody. They always want to have things their way – no self-sacrifice. They blame others for their ills. Our churches are filled with these immature Christians, who only want their way out of everything. Their slogans are always,
"Pray for me," but they do not take time themselves to pray or pray for others.
"My pastor does not visit me," but they've never blessed their pastor or visited him either.
"This person did this and that to me and so I am not going to church again." They forget that they are also not perfect, and there is no perfect church with all-perfect people anywhere.
"I do not like this pastor, or this deacon; this brother or this sister." They do not know the Word. The Word of God is against hatred and animosity towards each other.
There are many more excuses. They move from church to church, fellowship to fellowship, because they have not

trained themselves to stand trials, to grow in order to be of help to another person.

Growth always comes with pain. Pain when taking the first steps, and trying to walk with soggy diapers. In other words, they are not strong enough to stand on their own, let alone help others. They do not want to be refined, but in order to be useful in the Master's hand every believer must be willing to be refined.

Yes, fire make us mature and complete in Christ Jesus, and makes it possible to be an instrument of blessings to others.

It takes a mature person to mentor someone else. This generation needs mentors, and it is obvious the Lord is taking us through the fire to mother this young army He is raising up for this end-time revival.

The Bible also states in the same book of James and affirmed by the apostle John, that there is something better in store for us after the fires – the Crown of Life.

> "Blessed is the man who perseveres under trials, because when he has stood the test, he will receive the crown of life that God has promised to those who love Him" (James 1:12).
>
> "… Be thou faithful to the point of death, and I will give you the crown of life" (Rev. 2:10).

Daughter of the King, the Lord is taking or has taken you through the fire for some reasons. He knows He can trust you and me with anything. He knows He can make a covenant with us, and it shall not be broken. He knows you can carry out His plan of action in total obedience without wavering. He knows you will be ready for the next step of impacting others for the kingdom.

Catherine Jackson wrote, "We must meet our hurts, our disappointments, our frustrations, the malice of our enemies, the provoking habits of our friends—our trials and temptations of every sort – with an attitude of active and practical surrender and trust. Only then will we be able to spread our wings and fly above them all to the "heavenly places in Christ." From that vantage point we will be able to see our problems through the eyes of Jesus, and they will lose their power to harm or distress us."

ATTITUDE IN TRAINING - VERY IMPORTANT

Your attitude and mine through the fire 'training' determines what we actually want to become in the hand of the Almighty 'Goldsmith'. Either the fires will harden us and consume us, or it will perfect us for His glory. But if we can say with the Shunamite "All is well," even when we do not understand what He is doing, then His fires will refine and bring out the gold in us for His glory. He will toughen us to face all situations in life for the sake of His name.

Finally, the Apostle Paul establishes the fact that whatever happened to him was the advancement of the gospel (Philippians 1:12). Nothing happens to a child of God in vain.

> "Now I want you to know, brothers, that what has happened to me has really **served to advance the gospel**" (Philippians 1:12 – emphasis mine).

The Lord promised His presence in the fires! And he confirmed His word in the lives of the three Hebrew young men. Please read Isaiah chapter 43 and Daniel chapter 3.

I have been through lots of fires, and many times I have thought I have only charcoaled-burnt life left. But I have come to understand that God can use even our charcoaled-burnt life to bless others, because without charcoals there will be no more barbecues, and summer fun. Charles Swindoll says,

> "Learn your lessons well in the schoolroom of obscurity. God is preparing you as His chosen arrow. As yet your shaft is hidden in His quiver, in the shadows ... but at the précised moment at which it will tell with the greatest effect, He will reach for you and launch you to that place of His appointment."

Going through the fire is not easy, yet there is promotion after the fires! You and I are being prepared for the advancement of the kingdom. Do not throw in the towel. Look up! There is something good in the air!

QUOTABLE QUOTES

"There is no situation so chaotic that God cannot from that situation create something that is surpassingly good. He did it at creation. He did it at the cross. He is doing it today."

Bishop Handley Carr Glyn Moule (1841-1920)

[8]

WOMEN WHO HAVE BEEN THROUGH THE WATERS
(Transformation and Healing)

❖

"As the deer pants for streams of water, so my soul pants for you, O God. My soul thirst for God, for the living God. When can I go and meet with God? ... Deep calls to deep in the roar of Your waterfalls; all Your waves and breakers have swept over me. By day the Lord directs His love, at night His song is with me—a prayer to the God of my life" (Psalms 42:1-2, 7-8).

As said earlier, the goldsmith, after the fires, washes the gold or the silver in special water in order to beautify his product. Likewise after being refined by the fires, these end-time daughters of the King should be women who have been through the water of total transformation and healing; because His water will soothe the fire burnings. His water will clear up the old tissues on the burnt skin to make room for your beauty to glow.

- **Water figuratively speaks of spiritual growth.** "He is like a tree planted by the streams of water, which yields its fruit in season and whose leaf does not wither. Whatever he does shall prosper" (Psalms 1:3).
- **Water speaks of peace.** "He makes me to lie down in green pastures, he leads me beside quiet waters, he restores my soul" (Psalms 23:2-3).
- **Water speaks of the Christ and the Holy Spirit** (Ezekiel 47:1-12; John 4:10-15), **of regeneration** (John 7:37, 38), **of salvation** (Isaiah 55:1), and **of affliction** sometimes (Isaiah 43:2).

Water has so many significances and usages. According to scientists, water is a carrier of life, because it carries nutrients that enhance the human life. In the Bible, water is used for consecration; it is used for cleansing, for purification, for sanctification, and for baptism; but the Water the Lord spoke to me about is the Word of God and His Spirit.

Lack of natural water in the human body causes dehydration and lots of other ailments. Likewise, lack of spiritual water in our spiritual body will cause spiritual dehydration and lots of spiritual problems. There are many Christians who are spiritually dehydrated, because they do not drink enough of the spiritual water the Holy Spirit has provided.

What satisfies a hungry soul more than the Word of the Living God? What can make you effective in ministry other than the power of the Holy Spirit? Who can equip you to live a life well pleasing to the Lord more than the infilling of the Holy Spirit?

A) THE WATER OF THE UNADULTERATED WORD OF GOD

These end-time daughters of the King are women of the Word. They are women who spend time digging for the gold in the Word. The fire they have been through has created in them such great hunger and thirst for something greater and bigger than the offer of the world.

These are women who tremble at the Word of God. They are women who respect the Word and search through the Scriptures daily to know the mind of Christ and the will of the King for their lives.

Coming back to our Ruth lesson, don't you think Ruth was a woman of the Word? Ruth knew the Lord, and had the Word printed upon the tablet of her heart, confirming the words of the Lord in Luke 9:62.

> "And Jesus said unto him, 'No man having put his hand on the plough, and looking back, is fit for the kingdom" (Luke 9:62).

The Bible does not make mention with reference to Ruth reading the Bible, but her statement of affirmation to Naomi clearly points out that she knew the Word and the God of the Bible in a personal way. His Word was printed indelibly on her heart!

> "Entreat me not to leave thee, or to return from following after thee; for whither thou goest I will go;

and whither thou lodgest, I will lodge; thy people shall be my people and thy God my God; Where thou diest, I will die and there be buried: the Lord do so to me, and more also, if aught but death part thee and me" (Ruth 1:16-17).

THE INVITATION

The Bible says that at the last day of the feast in Jerusalem, Jesus cried passionately for men to come and drink this heavenly water (John 7:37), which signifies the Holy Spirit.

"On the final and climactic day of the Feast, Jesus took his stand. He cried out, "If anyone thirsts, let him come to me and drink. Rivers of living water will brim and spill out of the depths of anyone who believes in me this way, just as the Scripture says." (He said this in regard to the Spirit, whom those who believe in him were about to receive. The Spirit had not yet been given because Jesus had not been glorified" (John 7:37-38 – The Message).

When Jesus began His ministry, the first invitation He gave to mankind was the invitation to come and drink from the water or the fountain of Life freely. He gave the first cup to the woman at the well (John 4:1-15). Notice – He gave this spiritual water (The Word) to a woman — another mention of 'a' woman. This has great spiritual significance. Apart from the twelve disciples who were men, there were a lot of women who won the heart of the Master (Luke 8:2-3).

"Now he had to go through Samaria. So he came to a town in Samaria called Sychar, near the plot of ground Jacob had given to his son Joseph. Jacob's well was there, and Jesus, tired as he was from the journey, sat down by the well. It was about the sixth hour.

When a Samaritan woman came to draw water, Jesus said to her, "Will you give me a drink?" (His disciples had gone into the town to buy food.)

The Samaritan woman said to him, "You are a Jew and I am a Samaritan woman. How can you ask me for a drink? (For Jews do not associate with the Samaritans.)

Jesus answered her, "if you knew the gift of God and who it is that asks you for a drink, you would have asked him and he would have given you living water."

"Sir," the woman said, "you have nothing to draw with and the well is deep. Where can you get this living water?

Jesus answered, "Everyone who drinks this water shall thirst again, but whoever drinks the water I give him will never thirst. Indeed, the water I give him will become in him a spring of water welling up to eternal life.

The woman said to him, "Sir, give me this water so that I won't get thirsty..." (John 4:1-15 paraphrased). Please read also John 4:16-42.

The "No name Samaritan" was in a pool of despair. Her life was very miserable. She was going through another kind of fire, which may be either of her own making, or be as a result of childhood abuse. Who knows? Only God does. But as soon as the Truth penetrated into her hungry soul, she left her jar and, became a witness of Christ; and in just one day a whole village came to listen to Jesus. Jesus gave her a 'glass' of the Living Water she was thirsty for—the Word.

Daughters of the King, if we would be effective in the ministry of this end-time, we need to swim in the water of His presence - be women of the Word. Everything the Father has purposed for us is in His Word. We overcome the enemy with the Word, because the Word of God is our spiritual weapon to combat the lies of the enemy.

PAST RECORDS UNDER THE BLOOD

Having wrong foundations before coming to know the Lord, many of us need the Water (Word) to counteract the lies of the enemy that we do not have a testimony and can't be used of God. If God can use anything, even an animal to warn a prophet of impending danger, He can really use anything. Please, read Numbers 21:21-31.

The Lord does not screen into our past record in order to use us, as the world does before employing us; but your adversary does. The Lord does not remember your past wrong choices and the bad checks you wrote, but your accuser does. The Lord does not bring up the record of your past mistakes and confessed sins. They are all under the blood, but your enemy does. Your enemy's main motive is to distract you, to discourage you, and to beat you up until you crumble under your inability to resist him against anything. But the Lord has given you something greater than a bombshell that the enemy knows and fears — The Word of The Lord.

This was the very weapon our Lord and Master used to defeat his effort to deviate Him from accomplishing His divine purpose on earth. Our Lord's response to the enemy is, "It is written." If the Son of God defeated the enemy with the Word, we can also do the same, for it is written,

"And they overcame him by the blood of the Lamb and by the Word of their testimony" (Rev. 12:11).

Do you know the reason the Lord wants us to be in the Water of His Word? The first temptation the enemy used to topple the first woman and her husband was a lie to doubt the Word of the Lord. The devil's first attack was against the Word of the Lord, and he hasn't changed his tact. Rather he is intensifying his crafty ways in order to pull you away from the Word. The first woman did not have the written Word (the Bible) in hand – which is the whole counsel of God to mankind. She only heard one command, "Do not eat or you die." Praise God! We have the written published Word today. We are armed every day as we plunge ourselves in the Word of God.

Meditating on the Word of God is like jumping into the depth of the ocean. It's waves envelope every aspect of the individual; absorbing and saturating him or her with the knowledge of the Holy Spirit. The Word is living and active; it is powerful to do every good work in us. It goes beyond human reasoning. It penetrates through the tissues, the muscles, the bones and even the marrow. It is more active and powerful than any detergent, Clorox or power-drink I have ever seen (Heb 4:12-13). Because of the fiery experiences we have been through, our souls have received wounds that only the Word can heal.

> "For the word of God is quick, and powerful, sharper than any two edged sword, piercing even to the dividing asunder of soul and spirit, and of the joints and marrow, and is a discerner of the thoughts and intents of the heart. Neither is there any creature that is not manifest in his sight: but all things are naked and opened unto the eyes of him with whom we have to do" (Hebrews 4:12-13).

Many of us are still struggling with all the unresolved issues of our past and numerous unhealed hurts. Some of us are still dealing with past painful unimaginable experiences, and any time something happens similar to what we've been through, the wound is stirred up. Only the Word of God through the power of the Holy Spirit can perform such great surgery in order to bring total healing.

A wounded and dying soldier is of no or less benefit to any one. We are His recruits. Unless we dive deep into the Word, we cannot receive His healing, and without our own healing being completed, we cannot be of a help to anyone else. There are no 'fire burns' the Word cannot heal. The Bible says,

> "He sent His Word and healed them, and delivered them from their destructions" (Psalms 107:20).

Do you remember the centurion who came to Jesus for the healing of his servant? His request to Jesus was, *"Lord, speak only the Word and my servant shall be made whole"* (Please read Luke 7:1-10).

This Roman centurion knew the power of the spoken Word. Being an army officer or an army commander, he had experienced the power of words in the ordinary. He was able to command his subordinates in just few words and they obeyed. So he could discern to know that if Christ was who He claimed to be — the Son of God, then He could move in a higher realm of authority through the spoken Word than him. The Bible says,

> "..... The word is near you; it is in your mouth and in your heart; that is the word of faith we are proclaiming" (Roman 10:8).

How can we speak the Word out when the Word is not in us? How can we be healed when we do not have the spiritual medication, and do not know how to use the Word? How can we be His instruments of restoration and healing if the Word is not in us?

As a daughter of the King, the Word of God is your Father the King's love letter to you. In this letter, He has detailed all His plans, His desires, His purposes and His secrets. He has placed the keys that will unlock all these secrets of His heart, which the enemy stole from you in the beginning, in His love letter to you – the Bible. It contains the whole plan for your restoration. It contains the keys that will unlock your inheritance in Christ Jesus. The Word is His very heart to you.

May I ask you this question please? Have you read a part of this Love Letter today? If yes, do more, go deeper, for you are on your way to victory, but if not, no wonder the enemy is beating up on your head everyday with past hurt, past failures, threat of untimely death, fear of being a failure, and all his stinking arrows being thrown at you. The Lord Jesus, praying to the Father concerning His disciples, prayed that the Father would sanctify them by the Word. "Sanctify them through thy truth: thy word is truth" (John 17:17). His Word is a filth cleanser.

We are admonished by the Apostle Paul to be wise and redeem the time in this evil last days (Eph 5:14-17). But how can we attain such wisdom to fight against the enemy and his wiles when the Word has no place in our hearts? In Psalms 19, the Holy Spirit inspired King David to create thirst in us in order to become wise through His Word.

"The law (Word) of the Lord is perfect, reviving the soul. The statutes (Word) of the Lord are trustworthy, making wise the simple. The precepts (Word) of the Lord are right, giving joy to the heart. The commands (Word) of the Lord are radiant, giving light to the eyes. The fear of the Lord (Knowing and Living the Word) is pure, enduring forever. The ordinances (Word) of the Lord are sure and altogether righteous.

They are more precious than gold, than much pure gold; they are sweeter than honey, than the honey from the comb. By them is your servant warned; in keeping them there is great reward" (Psalms 19:7-11 emphasis mine).

It is so wonderful to see such great benefits of drinking the Living Water (the Word) in just these four verses of Psalms 19. The psalmist acknowledges this:

- The Word will revive and revitalize us to persevere in our walk with the Lord.
- The Word will make us wise, and the wise will always have the ability to discern the times and the seasons. We will know when to move and when not to.
- The Word will guide us. Read also Psalms 119:24. We will never live in confusion.
- The Word will give us joy unspeakable when the going gets tough, for His joy shall always be our strength.
- The Word will enlighten us. It will give us spiritual insights, and clarify our vision to see beyond our own capability.
- The Word becomes our only sure and righteous foundation that can never be shaken. It establishes us and enables us to live holy lives. The Word is our guide. It is our security checkpoint. It warns us of impending danger and keeps us from harm. And in keeping the Word, there is great reward.

DIFFERENT SYMBOLS OF THE WORD OF GOD

A hammer: It knocks out all indifferences and lawlessness. It breaks the hardhearted, and brings people to conviction.

"Is not My Word like fire," declares the Lord, and like a hammer that breaks a rock into pieces?" (Jeremiah 23:29).

A fire: It consumes wickedness and refines His children of all un-Christlikeness. It consumes all man-made creeds and extinguishes all disobedience.

"Therefore this is what the Lord God Almighty says: "Because the people have spoken these words, I will make My Words in your mouth a fire and these people the wood it consumes. ...."Is not My Word like fire, declares the Lord ..." (Jeremiah 5:14; Jeremiah 23:29).

A mirror: It reveals our true personality and character. Once you look at yourself in it, it stares you right in the face. Your image never leaves your memory; because it convicts men of who they really are—whether they like it or not.

"Do not merely listen to the Word, and so deceive yourself. Do what it says. Anyone who listens to the Word but does not do what it says is like a man who sees his face in a mirror and, after looking at himself (herself), goes away and immediately forgets what he looks like. But the man who looks intently into the perfect law that gives freedom, and continues to do this, not forgetting what he (she) has heard, but doing it—he (she) will be blessed in what he(she) does" (James 1:23 emphasis mine).

A seed: It penetrated deep down into the heart that reproduces life and transformation.

"For you have been born again, not of perishable seed, but of imperishable through the living and enduring Word of God. For, "All men are like grass, and all their glory is like the flower of the field, the grass withers and the flowers fall, but the Word of the Lord stands forever. And this is the Word that was preached to you" (I Peter 1:23-25). Please read also Matthew 13:1-23.

A deep well of water: The Word cleanses and purifies the believer. It is a well of water that never runs dry. It is always fresh.

"Husbands, love your wives, just as Christ loved the church and gave Himself up for her to make her holy, cleansing her by the washing with water through the Word, and to present her to Himself as a radiant church, without stain or wrinkle or any other blemish, but holy and blameless" (Ephesians 5:25-27 – Emphasis mine).

A lamp and a light: They brighten our paths and guide us from all the dark pitfalls of the enemy.

"Your Word is a lamp to my feet and a light for my path" (Psalms 119:105).
"The unfolding of Your words gives light; it gives understanding to the simple. ...Direct my foot-

steps according to your word; let not sin rule over me" (Psalms 119:130 & 133).

Rain and snow: They come down to renew, to restore, and flourish the soil of the believer's life, causing him or her to be fruitful, and to accomplish great things for the Kingdom.

"As the rain and the snow come down from heaven, and do not return to it without watering the earth and making it bud and flourish, so that it yields seed for the sower and bread for the eater, so is My Word that goes out from My mouth: It will not return to Me empty, but will accomplish what I desire and achieve the purpose for which I sent it" (Isaiah 55:10-11).

A sword: It penetrates deep into every part of the soul and the spirit, laying all intents of the heart bare before its Creator.

"For the Word of God is living and active. Sharper than any two edged sword, it penetrates even to dividing soul and spirit, joints and marrows, it judges the thoughts and the attitudes of the heart. Nothing in all creation is hidden from God's sight. Every thing is uncovered and laid bare before the eyes of him to whom we must give account" (Hebrews 4:12-13). Read James 4:12 and Ephesians 6:17.

The Word of God is precious than gold or silver that can enrich a believer for eternity (Psalms 19:7-10, Revelation 3:18). It is a super 'Electrical Power' which generates faith (Romans 10:17). It is a healing balm that brings healing, and it gives eternal life to the reader (Psalms 107:20, John 6:63). It is pure non-homogenized milk for spiritual babies (I Peter

2:2). It is whole grain bread for the hungry and good nutritional food to nourish the malnourished Christian (Matthew 4:4).

God uses His Word as a mighty weapon to take revenge against His enemies (Revelation 19:11-15). It is pure honey for the human soul (Psalms 19:10), and strong non-treated meat for matured men and women of God (Hebrews 5:11-14). It stands alone!

What a treasure we have in our Father's love letter to us! We have great assets in the Word! The Word of God is the only source of pure unadulterated water that can daily purify you and me, and prevents us from going back into our old lifestyles and conduct. Someone said: *"The Bible will keep you from sin and sin will keep you away from the Bible."* King David writes,

> "How can a young man (woman – daughter of the King) keep his (her) way pure? By living according to Your Word. ... I have hidden Your Word in my heart that I might not sin against You" (Psalms 119:9 and 11 - emphasis mine).

It is important for us to note also that the Word is our ultimate food for spiritual growth. Without the desire to eat and feed our souls with this unadulterated Word of God, we will never grow and come to the fulfillment of our destiny as daughters of the King.

*A TRIBUTE TO THE HOLY WORD OF GOD

The Bible is not an amulet, a charm, a fetish, or a book that will work wonders by its very presence. It is a book that will work wonders in every life, if acted upon and obeyed in faith and sincerity. The Bible reveals the mind of God, the state of man, the way of salvation, the doom of sinners, and the happiness of believers. Its doctrines are Holy. Its precepts are binding, its histories true and accurate, and its decisions immutable.

Read it to be wise, believe it to be safe, and practice it to be holy. The Bible is light to direct you, food to support you and comfort to cheer you. It is the traveler's map, the pilgrim's staff, the pilot's compass, the soldier's sword, and the Christian's charter. Here heaven is opened, and the gates of hell disclosed. Christ is its grand subject (central theme), our good is its design, and the glory of God its end. It should fill your memory, rule your heart, and guide your feet in righteousness and true holiness. Read it slowly, frequently, prayerfully, meditatively, searchingly, devotionally, and study it constantly, perseveringly, and industriously. Read it through and through until it becomes part of your being and generates faith that will move mountains.

The Bible is a mine of wealth, the source of health, and a world of pleasure. It is given to you in this life. It will be opened at the judgment, and will stand forever. It involves the highest responsibility, will reward the least to the greatest of labor, and will condemn all who trifle with its sacred contents.

*WHAT GREAT MEN HAVE SAID ABOUT THE BIBLE

"It is impossible to rightly govern the world without God and the Bible" (George Washington).

"A studious perusal of the Sacred Volume will make better citizens, better fathers, and better husbands" (Thomas Jefferson).

"The Bible is the first and almost the only Book deserving of universal attention" (John Quincy Adams).

"It is the Rock on which our Republic stands" (Andrew Jackson).

"A man has deprived himself of the best there is in the whole world who has deprived himself of this—a knowledge of the Bible" (Woodrow Wilson).

"There is no other book so various as the Bible, nor one so full of concentrated wisdom" (Herbert Hoover).

"To the influence of this Book we are indebted for the progress made in civilization, and to this we must look as our guide in the future" (Ulysses S. Grant).

"What can I do with respect to the next world without my Bible?" (John Bacon).

"The Bible is more than a Book; it is a living being with an action; a power which invades everything that opposes its extension" (Napoleon Bonaparte).

"All other books are of little importance in comparison with the Bible" (Alexander Cruden).

"The Bible is the Book of faith, and a Book of doctrine, and a Book of morals, and a Book of religion, of special revelation from God; but it is also a Book which teaches man his responsibility, his own dignity, and his equality with fellow men" (Daniel Webster).

*(Taken from Dake Annotated Study Bible)

B) THE LIVING WATER OF THE HOLY SPIRIT

"…. I saw water coming out from under the threshold of the temple toward the east (for the temple faced east). The water was coming down from under the south side of the temple, south of the altar. And the water was flowing from the south. …..He led me through water that was ankle deep. … He led me through water that was knee deep. … and led me through water that was up to the waist. He measured off another thousand, but now it was a river that I could not cross, because the water had risen and was deep enough to swim in — a river that no one could cross" (Ezekiel 47:1-6).

Israel's sin led them into captivity. Calamities of various judgments the Lord brought upon them were so appalling, the name of the Lord was even profaned among the Gentile nations that took them captive. In the midst of all this profanity against the Holy one of Israel, God in His mercies, and for the sake of His Holy name, promised restoration to His people through the water – clean water to cleanse and remove all the pollutions and impurities from them.

Through this process, Israel shall be transformed, be given a new heart and a new Spirit, as He removes the heart of stone; replacing it with a malleable, supple heart of flesh, enabling the Holy Spirit to take His rightful place in their lives. At this point, Israel will be ready to obey His command fully (Ezekiel 39:24-27).

God is ready in these last hours of the church, not only to sprinkle clean water upon those of us whose lives are, or have been shattered because of whatever happened to us; directly or indirectly. He is ready to plunge us, and immerse us deeply in the river of His presence, and of His power, to remove our shame; to defend our case and to restore us for HIS HOLY NAME sake. Teresa of Avila said,

> "If then, you sometimes fall, do not lose heart. Even more, do not cease striving to make progress from it, for even out of your fall, God will bring some good."

In this Ezekiel prophetic experience of the water, which the angel showed him, we see clearly through the eye of the Spirit the different dimensions of an encounter with the Holy Spirit.

We don't want an ankle deep experience. We want neither knee nor waist experiences. We must yearn and desire a spiritual renewal that comes from an-all-out, deep immersed, saturated experience of God's power and glory, which will enable us to bring glory to His holy name through our fruitfulness. Ray C. Stedman, in his book Adventure through Daniel, Ezekiel and Revelation wrote,

> "God has chosen to dwell within the human spirit. That spirit was made to be a holy of holies in which the living God takes up residence. The secret of a rich, full satisfying life, a life of genuine excitement and continuing significance – is to live by the limitless resources of the Holy Spirit of God" (pg 13).

We are the Living Temples of the Holy Spirit, through which God wants to demonstrate His power. We are His Living Sanctuaries into which He desires to pour His life. We must be careful how we disparage this temple's value. It was bought with a great price; the Life and the blood of the only Begotten Son of the Living God!

> "… Do you not know that your body is the temple of the Holy Spirit who is in you, whom you have from God, and you are not your own? For you were bought with a price; therefore glorify God in your body and in your spirit, which are God's" (I Corinthians 6:19-20).

The Holy Spirit values us more than what we can even imagine. Humans are the only instruments through which God's glory will be manifested to the world. We need to take a deeper plunge into this Living water.

SWIMMING IN THE RIVER

From this passage in Ezekiel chapter 47, we see the end result of a life that has fully plunged into the Spirit's Living water. The river of living water, flowing from the Spirit of God to our spirit is the only purifying stream, which can remove all the pollution and staleness from our lives. It is the source of true transformation of every individual believer, and the only power in the life of a Christian that can cause one to be fruitful. (Read Ezekiel 47:7-12).

In the first place, rivers of Living Water will flow from the heart of Christ to ours; purifying and transforming our lives. Secondly, the soil of our lives will be fertile for reproduction and fruitfulness. Then through us, He will flow to fill hungry souls. Through us, He will heal wounded hearts. Through us, the weak will receive strength. Through us, the hurting will find peace and solace, and the dying will be revived; because out of us shall flow rivers of living waters as Christ said.

> "Whoever believes in Me, as the Scripture has said, streams of living water will flow from within him." By this He meant the Spirit, whom those who believed in Him were later to receive. ..." (John 7:38).

There are so many fanatics and spiritual crooks today that when one begins to speak concerning the Holy Spirit, many close their ears, especially when speaking of tongues is mentioned. Please, I assure you, I am not going to speak about tongues now, so continue the reading of this message.

This message is about being clothed with the Holy Spirit and living the Spirit life. It is God who is calling us into this ministry of the end-time to be His able ministers of the New Covenant. Ultimately this ministry is not going to function through human endeavors or human wisdom, but through that of the Spirit of the Lord according to the prophet Joel.

"And it shall come to pass afterwards, that I will pour out my spirit upon all flesh; and your sons and your daughters shall prophesy ..." (Joel 2:28).

The prophet's message in this verse commences with, "*And it shall come to pass that afterwards,*" which denotes a precedence of something or an event. Israel had fallen away from the Lord and had been devastated by her enemy. The enemy through subtlety like the palmerworm entered their camp, grieving the heart of the Father. He gradually grew to be the caterpillar, and then into the cankerworm, and stripped Israel of her freedom. He finally invaded the whole land with full grown locusts and brought drought, according to Joel, and took them to captivity.

Prophet Joel summoned the people to repentance, which was going to bring about their restoration if they met the condition of obedience laid out by the Lord. About that time, the Spirit of the Lord poured out power and supernatural abilities on the people as they saw their enemies destroyed.

Although these things happened in Joel's time, do you see the same problem in our society today? Yes and even worse. Our generation is drifting gradually into hell, and without God's intervention, nothing good will definitely come out. But there is hope. We are His instruments of restoration, and this is the reason the Holy Spirit is calling you, daughter of the King to enter into covenant with Him.

You see, the disciples did not commence their ministry to the world, beginning from Jerusalem, until they obeyed the command of the Master to wait until they were endued with power from on high. Didn't they walk with the Master for three years? Yes. Weren't they sent to preach to the household of Israel? That's true. Weren't they able to heal the sick and cast out demons? Of course!

Do you know that these experiences Jesus shared with His disciples were still under the old covenant, because Christ had not fulfilled the law yet through His death? Under the old covenant people received healings. Under the old covenant miracles happened. Under the old covenant people saw the glory of God, but the glory of the new covenant under the commonwealth of the Holy Spirit is much more glorious.

> "Now if the ministry that brought death, which was engraved in letters on stone, came with glory, so that the Israelites could not look steadily at the face of Moses because of its glory, fading though it was, will not the ministry of the Spirit be even more glorious?" (2 Corinthians 3:7-8).

This was the reason Jesus said, "In this rejoice not... but rejoice that your names are written in the book of life" (Luke 10:20). Jesus was trying to convey to them the important message concerning the blessedness of the new covenant. In other words, He is saying to the disciples: *"When you get your name inscribed in heaven, you become a candidate for greater inheritances and greater works; so I am giving you power over all the powers of the enemy, and nothing can touch or harm you. But you can only get the fullness of this experience when you tarry in Jerusalem until you are saturated with power from on high."*

After the resurrection, didn't Jesus breathe the Holy Spirit on them? Yes, and I believe this gesture gave them a foretaste of what it would be like receiving the fullness of the Holy Spirit on the day of Pentecost.

Look at the lives of the apostles before the Spirit came upon them. There was envy and jealousy among them. Some were even fighting as regards to who would be the greatest. Get the picture clearly here? They were with Jesus Himself. They had wonderful firsthand experience of living, eating, sleeping and walking with God becoming flesh. Yet they had tough times in their walk with the Lord. It took the plenitude of the Holy Spirit for them to turn their world right side up.

Can you imagine coward Peter, who denied Christ three times, preaching on the day of Pentecost and converting three thousand souls? Can you figure out how this same Peter could stand in front of the Jewish Sanhedrin and confess boldly, "We must obey God rather than men."?

What transformed Peter from being a coward to a mighty anointed evangelist whose shadow healed the sick? It was the Holy Spirit. Can you imagine this same Peter being scolded by Paul for showing partiality, yet did not fight back? Praise God! It is the Holy Spirit in action in his life.

A PERSONAL EXPERIENCE

All those who knew me before do not comprehend how the Lord has transformed me from being shy and cowardly into a preacher of righteousness. I remember my third son Samuel, calling his brothers and making this remark, when he heard me preach, *"Mama is a different person when the anointing comes upon her. I could not believe my eyes when I saw the soft-spoken shy mother, preaching with such tenacity."* Glory to the Lord! This is what the Holy Spirit can do in the life of a true believer of Christ drinking unceasingly the water of His presence.

How many believers do we have in our world today who read the Bible and yet do not understand it? It is the Holy Spirit, who quickens the Word in the heart of a reader to comprehend what the Father is communicating to them; for the carnal mind cannot comprehend the things of the Spirit because they are spiritually discerned. The Lord Jesus said,

"The Spirit gives life; the flesh counts for nothing. The words I have spoken to you are spirit and they are life" (John 6:63).

Without the Holy Spirit quickening the Word in our innermost being, in our spirits' mind, everything we read will be short-lived or meaningless. He turns on the light of clear illumination of the Word in our spirit. So the Holy Spirit and the Word go together. They do because the Word was written through the inspiration of the Holy Spirit. He is the author of the Bible.

"All Scripture is God-breathed and is useful for teaching, rebuking, correcting and training, in righteousness, so that the man (woman) of God may be thoroughly equipped for every good work. ... For prophecy never had its origin in the will of men, but men spoke from God as they were carried along by the Holy Spirit" (2 Timothy 3:16-17; 2 Peter 1:21).

The apostle Paul also affirms the words of the Lord Jesus in saying that the letter kills but the Spirit gives life.

"He has made us competent as ministers of a new covenant – not of the letter but of the Spirit; for the letter kills, but the Spirit gives life" (2 Corinthians 3:6).

You need the Baptism of the Holy Spirit. Like the disciples, the Trinity came to live in you when you gave your life to Jesus. But now you need the fullness of the Holy Spirit.

In the natural, it takes the fusion of the husband's sperms and the egg of the wife to birth life into this world. When the child begins to grow, he or she needs to experience the fullness of their own personality – body, soul and spirit, to understand and enjoy the life God has given him or her. In the same way, it took the effort of the Triune God to make you a child of God, but it takes the full, complete experience of the baptism and the fullness of the Holy Spirit in every individual Christian's life to understand and enjoy the real Christian life and its benefits.

"Until we have taken that plunge, life is nothing but a plodding, dogged, difficult path full of frustrations and spiritual defeat," says Ray Stedman. "When we immerse ourselves in the mighty, gushing torrent of the rivers of Living water, once the Spirit of God flows through us and over us like a rushing, life giving river, then the entire Christian life begins to make sense" (Adventure through the Bible).

You and I are also triune beings. We have bodies that are only the vehicles carrying our spirits and our soul. As you know, our souls consist of our wills, our mind and our emotions, but our spirit is that which connects us to God. Your spirit is the life of God in you, who yearns to fellowship with God. You are a spirit being who needs a higher spiritual power to capture the soul's ability to dominate your life. That is another reason why we need the Baptism of the Holy Spirit. (It has been explained fully why we need an intimacy with the Holy Spirit in the next two texts following). When the Holy Spirit comes in His fullness into your life,

- He will impart spiritual gifts to you. (1 Corinthians 12:1-11)
- He will bond you together with other believers because we all belong to Him. (1 Corinthians 12:12-26, Ephesians 4:1-2)
- He will speak mysteries through you. (1 Corinthian 14:2, Ephesians 3:4-5)

- He will help you in your prayer life. Your prayer life will be more effective. (Romans 8:26-27)
- He changes our lives and imparts the character of Christ into us. (2 Corinthians 3:18, Galatians 5:22)
- He strengthens our inner man, and equips us for effective ministry. (Ephesians 3:16-19, 4:4-16)
- The Holy Spirit equips us to be faithful witnesses. (Acts 1:8, 2:1-40)
- The Holy Spirit is the source of true harvest. We cannot be effective in soul winning in this end-time ministry without the indwelling Holy Spirit. (John 4:34-36, Acts 1:8)

Dear sister, open your mouth wide and let Him fill you up.

QUOTABLE QUOTES

"The Spirit-filled life is not a special, deluxe edition of Christianity. It is part and parcel of the total plan of God for His people."

A W. Tozer (1897-1963)

[9]

WOMEN WHO HAVE ENTERED INTO THE KING'S CHAMBER

(Intimacy and Revelation)

❖

"All glorious is the princess within her chamber, her gown is interwoven with gold. In embroidered garment she is led to the King. ..." (Psalms 45:14-15).

"Take me away with you – Let us hurry! Let the King bring me into His chambers. We rejoice and delight in You; we will praise Your love more than wine. How right they are to adore you" (Song of Solomon 1:4).

It takes the Word and the Spirit to really fall in love with Jesus. If you are now eating at His table, His Word is purifying you, strengthening you, and preparing you for greater things. And if you are drinking from His fountain, His Holy Spirit is calling you, drawing you now into His inner chamber.

Do you know why some of us have such strong appetite for non-nutritional foods and sodas to the point where it has become very hard for some to go a day without a coke? Do you know why we have such a craving for sweets and chocolates? Any ways, lack of appetite for good foods is also as dangerous as excessive appetite for what we do not need.

Do you know why some of us have become shopaholics? We shop and shop and shop until the last dime is spent and yet we are not satisfied. Then we begin preparing for yard sales in order to get rid of the old and start all over again to shop and to shop. It is not a physical hunger. It is not just a natural craving or a desire to have and to own. It is the wooing of the Spirit drawing you into a deeper relationship with the King as said earlier. He is still taking some through the fire, through the Word, and into a Holy Ghost super Baptism for His glory.

Our Heavenly Father, the King, desires to have an intimate relationship with us, and you are a candidate. Do you know the reason for our candidacy? It is because of our acceptance of His sacrifice. It is because He called us to Himself, and for Himself. He chose you for His own. He has His seal upon your life. He has taken you through the fire to remove the dross off you. Now He wants us to get intimate. The door to the inner chamber is wide open because of the blood.

REAL INTIMACY

The inner chamber of the King illustrates intimacy. Real intimacy between a husband and a wife does not happen in front of people, not even before any of their own children. It occurs behind closed doors. It occurs when every distraction is set aside. It is just between the lovers.

Many Christians are only used to church fellowship and prayer meetings. They mistakenly or ignorantly confuse these with a personal and intimate relationship with the Lord. These activities are very good, but not the best, for if there are no fellowships or prayer centers in the future, where will your foundation be? Or if you one day find yourself in a place where there are no church folks around to pray with you, how will you survive?

Christians in Muslim and communist nations have not the privileges we have today in our free world. Some cannot even attend church services, yet they are firm in their convictions about Christ and His Word. They are still strong in their daily walk with the Lord, more than some of us who have all the liberty to do so. Each day, some of these persecuted saints, step into eternity with pain and scars on their bodies. I believe the secret of their willingness to die for the sake of Christ is the deep intimacy they have with the Lord.

TODAYS MARRIAGES

Many of the King's daughters are like marriages we see today in our world. On the surface, many presume all is well. On the outside, we see them as wonderful and perfect couples, but in their inner chamber, they are not really intimate. They fuss at each other and complain, and they even resent one another many times. Although they live under the same roof and sleep on the same bed, their hearts are far-flung from one another. They are married, yet not bonded.

Most of these struggling couples, give flimsy excuses as to why their marriages are being tossed about, but a closer look into those relationships give you a clear understanding of their problem—they are not really intimate with God and with one another.

One may be a workaholic or a slave to television. The other is just hanging around just for the sake of the children. Their intimacy has been sacrificed for something else. You see, marriage is a school. No one graduates from learning life's lessons. It takes us to the grave—likewise our relationship with the Lord.

The saying that 'familiarity breeds contempt', is really true. Familiarity breeds disrespect. Before we came to know the Lord, we knew there was something missing in our lives. Then the grace of God appeared to us. We embraced Christ. As the hunger to know Him more than ever was sparked and rekindled in our spirits, we really fell in love with Jesus. Prayer was fun. The reading of the Word was like a magnet that drew us into intimacy with the Lord. However, with time, and the busyness of our lives, the zeal waned away; the fire began to die down, and the 'love life' we had with Christ in the past, has now become 'familiar—one of those things' we do not value any longer. Prayer is now a chore to some of us. As for the Word, it had become like one of those 'undesirable' desserts we pick up at the groceries once in while to satisfy our craving.

Brethren, we cannot relate well to men if we are not in deep relationship with God. A deeper intimacy with the Lord enables one to love in spite of, because God does love us in spite of our capriciousness toward Him. You can impress people by being far away, but we can only impact people by being close to them. The examples of Abraham and Joseph are worthy of emulation.

No matter what happened between Lot and Abraham, which led to their separation, Abraham sought after him and delivered him and his family from slavery. Through Abraham's intercession, Lot was spared from Sodom. Everywhere Abraham went, whether with good or bad pagan kings, God's love and character beamed out through him. Even in the midst of his fears, anxiety, and sometimes mistakes, he exhibited the love of God to his adversaries. He was very intimate with the Lord. No wonder he was called the friend of God.

Just ponder on what Joseph went through. Whether it was slavery, ill treatment, imprisonment or what, it all resulted to the fact that his brothers hated and despised him for his dreams and good character. Yet Joseph could boldly say before his brothers, "You meant it for evil but God meant it for good."

> "… Do not be distressed and do not be angry with yourselves for selling me here, because it was to save lives that God sent me ahead of you. …" (Genesis 45:5).

He forgave them, and sought for their good all the days of his life. What was the secret? It was the result of deeper intimacy with the Lord.

There are many Christians who are just hanging around in the church for the sake of not being labeled backsliders or unbelievers. But deep down in their hearts, the desire to pray and to eat fresh manna from the Lord is no longer there. They are spiritually exhausted. Please, fall in love with Jesus.

KNOWING WHO THE FATHER IS

An intimate relationship with the Lord goes deeper than fellowship or church prayer meetings. It goes beyond group fellowship or cell groups. It is a personal encounter with the Beloved through prayer. (I have devoted a whole chapter on

Prayer). Intimacy brings you into knowing your Heavenly Father more intimately than ever. You will know that He is a real Father to You. You will not have head knowledge regarding who He is. Rather, you will experience and live out who He is in your personal life everyday as He reveals Himself to you. You will know Him in a different perspective. The Lord will truly be known as your,

- **Jehovah Jireh** – "And my God will meet all your needs according to His glorious riches in Christ Jesus" (Philippians 4:19). Read also Genesis 22:14, Matthew 6:25-34. No need in your life can break you into pieces. He always shows up just at the right time to meet every need.
- **Jehovah Rapha** – "If you listen carefully to the voice of the Lord your God and do what is right in His eyes, if you pay attention to his commands and keep all His decrees, I will not bring on you any of the diseases I brought on the Egyptians, for I am the Lord who heals you" (Exodus 15:26). Doctors may declare you hopeless however, because you have known the Great Healer to be who He is, you will believe in His faithfulness to heal you (Jeremiah 17:14; 1 Peter 2:24-25).
- **Jehovah Shalom** – (Judges 6:23, 24, Ephesians 2:14, Philippians 4:7). He becomes your peace when all things around you begin to shake and fall apart. Even when tears run down your cheeks, your heart just rests in peace, for you know deep in your heart He is in control.
- **Jehovah Nissi** – (Exodus 17:15-16; Isaiah 54:14-17). No power stands against you and survives. He is, and becomes your protector and your Victor. He literary fights all your battles for you, because He is mighty in battle!

- **Jehovah Ra'ah** – The Lord your shepherd (Psalms 23). He will take your hand and direct your footsteps. No path of yours will be your own undertaking but His. And when you become tired and weary, He will pick you up, and give you strength to continue your walk with Him.
- **Jehovah Tsidkenou** – The Lord our righteousness. When the enemy comes to you, accusing you and reminding you of your past, you can boldly testify of what Christ has done for you and in you; declaring you are righteous through Him. You no longer live under condemnation because of Christ. You have been justified and acquitted through faith in Christ Jesus our Lord (Romans 5:1, Romans 8:1-2).
- **El-Shaddai** — You will need nothing (2 Corinthians 9:8-11). He is our all sufficient God and Father. He fills every area of our being. He is more than enough to you.

Nothing changes your position of trust to doubt. Nothing changes your firm foundation of an unfeigned love and faith to that of unbelief. Yes, because you have known Him intimately, and during this time of closeness He reveals who Jesus Christ really is to you.

INTIMACY WITH THE SPIRIT

The Father has betrothed us to the Son, and as we go deeper into knowing the Father, we are drawn into deep intimacy with our spouse, who is our Lord and Savior Jesus Christ through the Holy Spirit, and to others. Do you remember the promise the Lord Jesus gave concerning the coming of the Holy Spirit? He said the Holy Spirit would receive of Him (Jesus) and show it to us.

"But when the Comforter is come, whom I will send unto you from the Father, even the Spirit of Truth, which proceeds from the Father, He shall testify of Me" (John 15:26).

"Howbeit when He, the Spirit of truth is come, He will guide you into all truth for He shall not speak of himself; but whatsoever He shall hear, that shall He speak; and He will show you things to come. He shall glorify Me; for He shall receive of Mine, and shall show it unto you. All things that the Father hath are Mine; therefore said I, that He shall take of Mine, and shall show it unto you" (John 16:13-15).

According to the reference we just read about the coming of the Holy Spirit we see the following benefits of having an intimacy with the Lord:

v **His presence brings insight and spiritual knowledge**

"But when He, the Spirit of truth, comes ... He will take from what is mine and make it known to you."

He will be known not just as a Savior but as Lord; the One who demands our all. He does not want a partial intimacy, He wants a deeper intimacy that requires me to forget about myself and yield to His ultimate will and desires. He is a spouse who does not share His bride with any other and such is our intimacy with the Lord.

You see, when Thomas saw the Lord personally, He got a direct revelation of His Lordship and His Deity, as he proclaimed "My Lord and my God" (John 20:24-28). When we go deeper into the inner chamber, all our doubts and unbelief will be erased by the power of His presence.

v   **His presence brings guidance.**

"But when He, the Spirit of truth, comes …. … He will guide you into all truth."

You will know the will of the Lord, and what He expects from you, because He will guide you into all the truth. How can you know the truth about your inheritance in Christ Jesus and enjoy the benefits of these inheritances without such an intimacy?

There was a story about a king who had great wealth. I mean billions of dollars and precious jewels. He divided his inheritance between his two children and placed their names on each of their inheritances. The younger one, who was closer to the father, knew what his share was, and started enjoying the part that was reserved for him. The other one, who never was close to the father, and lived far away from the family, lived like a pauper for years until he decided one day to go back home to develop a closer relationship with the father. When the news got to the father regarding his son standing behind the gate and wanting to come in, 'Daddy Rich' had a heart attack from overwhelming joy on seeing his son again.

Due to his sickness, he could not speak to his son before he passed away. The younger brother never showed him his part of the inheritance. Even though big brother came home to the father, he did not have a clue as to what his father had prepared in advance for him. He still lived in ignorance, because his brother was the intermediary between him and the inheritance. As it happened, this young man had to share his part of the inheritance with his brother, because he did not know the truth about what the father had provided for him. He got a quarter of his father's treasures.

Like the young man in the story, many Christians today are sharing (dividing) their inheritance with others because they do not know what theirs is. They are only feasting on someone else's revelation and dream and not on their own experience or personal encounter with the Lord. Your inheritance is tailor-made. It came with the package of salvation. It is post-marked with your name on it. Get closer to the Lord and the Holy Spirit will show you all things.

v His presence brings revelation

"But when He, the Spirit of truth, comes ……. He will tell you what is yet to come."

He will reveal all His secrets to you. Psalms 25:14 declares, *"The secret of the Lord is with them that fear him, and he will show them his covenant."* It is because of the intimacy I have cultivated with the Lord that He began to reveal things about the end-time daughters to me. I am not what I want to be, but it is so amazing to hear the Lord call me by name, and speaks to me concerning what He is about to do in the end-time. I am humbled to be one of His servants to write down these messages to His daughters.

I can't tell you how many wonderful things He has revealed to me – secrets of the enemy, global issues, and many more. The tragedy on September 11, 2001 was revealed to me in April 2001. The Lord spoke to me about a horrible tragedy that was going to happen to this nation because people have not given Him His rightful place in this nation. He said to me, "This event would be a warning sign for this nation to turn around and come back to Me. ..." The Lord also revealed to me how the intercessors (watchmen and women) He placed in this nation were sleeping. All these revelations He gave me were part of the confirmation concerning His calling upon my life to leave Africa, and arrive here before the borders of the United States became tight.

Many times I would wake up in the night to find a pen and a paper to write down His heart's cry to all of us. At the present, I always have a pen and a notepad by my bed. The Father's Heart Ministries Handbook and God Still Speaks (Divine Alphabet For Breakthrough), and all the books and songs He is leading me to write are all a direct result of Him speaking to me.

"Surely the Lord will do nothing, but He revealeth His secrets unto His servants the prophets" (Amos 3:7).

v   The King's presence brings favor.

"Even to the half of my kingdom, I will give it to you" (Esther 5:6, 7:2)

There was something about Esther that made the king desire to see her the second and third time until her enemies were destroyed. Her first approach to king took prayer and fasting. But when she found favor with him the first time, the rest became easy.

Going into His presence the first time is hard. It needs a strong desire to cultivate intimacy, but once access is restored through perseverance, it is easy to enhance your relationship. He longs to share Himself with us. He yearns to see you. He yearns to hear your voice and commune with you. He yearns to share His treasures with us. He loves to give us the kingdom.

You see, even this earthly king Ahasuerus, told Esther, "Even to the half of my kingdom, I will give it to you" (Esther 5:6, 7:2 paraphrased). What about the Creator of the universe who has now become your Father? Please read the book of Ephesians and Colossians. These two letters the Holy Spirit wrote through the Apostle, is a wonderful eye-opening tool for the believer into knowing the great inheritance we have in Christ Jesus.

v The King's presence brings transformation.

"His face shone like the sun, and His clothes became as white as the light" (Matthew 17:2).

Do you know what His presence can do in your life? You will shine like a princess. Your face will glow with his glory. You will walk through life with boldness and power because His stamp of approval is on your life.

In a moment, Ruth changed from a Moabite to Jewish. She changed from a foreigner into a queen mother in Israel. She changed from a widow without children to a blessed mother of Israel..

Do you know what the presence of the Lord has done in my life? He's changed me from being timid and shy into giving me boldness to preach His Word. He's taken away my fears, my sense of worthlessness, and is making me strong each day like a 'bolt,' fixed on Christ and never shaken. He's given me the ability to write books and compose songs, which in the natural wouldn't have been possible. All that I am today and hope to be in future is a direct result of Who He is to me.

v The King's presence leads to Christlikeness.

"Be imitators of God, therefore, as dearly loved children and live a life of love, just as Christ loved us and gave Himself up for us as a fragrant offering and sacrifice to God" (Ephesians 5:1-2).

We will be clothed with the character and the beauty of the Lord. It has been said that if couples are really intimate and are bonded together for a long time, they begin to resemble each other. Physically, this seems to happen to some people; and in so many ways, they begin to act and do things alike.

Obviously, God's ultimate purpose in saving you and me, and His ultimate goal is for us to be like Jesus. All those who have walked intimately with Him have experienced this beauty of character. It is not enough to quote II Corinthians, chapter five verses seventeen, there is more to that. It is the character of Christ in us that will draw souls to the kingdom, and if we are going to be a part of this army for revival, Christ **must** be seen in us (Philippians 2:5-16).

All fathers and mothers are proud to hear people comparing their children to them because somehow they resemble them in a good way. God the Father was very proud to testify about Jesus, "This is My beloved Son in whom I am well pleased. Hear ye Him."

I also felt my Heavenly Father was somehow proud about me this day, even though I did not feel that way about myself. I was sitting beside a lady who was driving me to Mobile to speak at the Women's Aglow meeting. There were three of us in this truck. The other two were very excited when they picked me up, but as we continued our trip, there was total silence. I became somehow very nervous, thinking they might have been disappointed to pick up a real black African minister. However, my speculation was wrong. Somewhere arriving near the place of ministry, I asked the reason for their silence. They sat and sighed for while, and then one of them said, "We were awed by the presence of the Lord as you entered this truck. I feel so dirty before the anointing that is present here right now." Believe me; that statement humbled me, because I know I am just a graced (favored) saint trying always to reach higher into His presence.

v **Intimacy with the King changes one's life and perspective completely.**

He clothes us with humility to accept His will for our lives in any circumstance. As a result of this impartation, we become willing vessels like Christ to be where He wants us to be and to do what He wants us to do in whatever state we may find ourselves. As we desire to become more and more like Jesus every day, we are clothed with humility, submissiveness, obedience, a gentle spirit, and the very desire to be like Christ each day. The book of Philippians states,

> "Let this mind be in you, which was also in Christ Jesus; who being in the form of God, thought it not robbery to be equal with God, but made himself of no reputation and took upon him the form of a servant, and was made in the likeness of men; And being found in fashion as a man he humbled himself, and became obedient unto death, even the death of the cross" (Philippians 2:5-8).

v **His presence produces a life of deep respect for God and love for human beings.**

When you read the letters of Paul, you will discover that he wrote them with deep reverence for the One who called him into this ministry of reconciliation. He had also deep 'fatherly' love for the converts he was discipleling (Acts 20:17-37).

Moses had the same experience. Israel had sinned. God wanted to destroy all of them and start all over with Moses and his descendants as His new nation. Moses, in awe of what the Lord was going to do, cried and pleaded for the people; making mention that if God refused to forgive the people, He should blot his (Moses') name out of His book (Exodus 32 & 33).

Our Heavenly Daddy, the King, yearns to be with you alone in order to communicate His heart with you, and to reveal what He has for you personally. He does not need any intermediary. Intermediaries interfere with the line of communication between Him and us. Intermediaries may give you the wrong information or misrepresent the truth of His heart to you. All He wants is you and me. I love this song very much.

> Take me into the Holy of Holies
> Take me by the blood of the Lamb
> Take me into the Holy of Holies
> Take the coals – cleanse my lips, here I am.

Let's just take a look at some examples from the Bible of some, who met the Lord face to face when they were alone.

Abraham —The Lord took him out from the family 'fellowship level' in Haran in order to solidify His covenant with him. As long as his father was around, Abraham could not move forward (Genesis 11:31-32, 12:1-8). As long as Lot was around him, Abraham never reached the peak of his destiny, and he did not hear the voice of the Lord again until Lot left. Lot was taken out of the way for him to experience a full encounter with the Lord of the covenant. And Abraham became a friend of God. The Bible says,

> "The Lord said to Abram **after Lot had parted from him**, "Lift up your eyes from where you are and look north and south, east and west. All the land that you see I will give to you and your offspring forever. ..."
> (Genesis 13:14-18).

Jacob — He had been running away from his brother for cheating. Next, he was going back home, also running away from his father-in-law, because Laban cheated him too. Jacob was a runner. He then heard of the arrival of his brother to meet him. Gripped by fear, he went away from his family to spend time with the Lord. Jacob wrestled with the Angel of the Lord till daybreak (Genesis 32:22-31). His perseverance in prayer turned Jacob's life around forever. He left the presence of God with a new name, a new heart and a new personality. God always leaves His fingerprint on any life that gets close to Him.

Joseph – Before the Lord elevated Joseph, He took him away from the family in order to perfect his character, and to prepare him to be the 'savior' of his family. Although he went through terrible trials, everywhere Joseph served, the presence of God reflected on his behavior, on his decision-making, and on his surroundings. It was recorded,

> "And the Lord was with Joseph, and he was a prosperous man; and he was in the house of his master the Egyptian. And his master saw that the Lord was with him, and that the Lord made all that he did to prosper in his hand" (Genesis 39:2-3).

Joseph, as we all know was a type of Christ. Please Genesis chapters 37, 39 to 45.

Moses — Wanting to do things his way did not work. The Lord in His Sovereignty took him away from Egypt to the desert in order to teach him how to shepherd His people. It was when he was alone without the daughters of Jethro and his family that the Lord appeared. Seeing the fire without the bush burning up, aroused his curiosity to go near. The Lord met him and equipped him to be the leader and deliverer of His people (Exodus 2:11-25; 3 & 4).

Later on, as they journeyed toward Canaan, Moses went before the presence of the Lord on the mountain many times. The Lord wanted to commune with His people, but the people of Israel were not ready or willing to do so. Moses' encounter with the Lord on the mountain transformed him completely. When he came down from the mountain, the populace could not look at his face. He had to veil up his face before communicating with the people. Moses became the meekest man on earth.

Joshua met the Captain of the Host of the Lord before crossing Jordan to conquer Jericho. He received precise instructions, and supernatural strategy to destroy Jericho. The victory came because He had an encounter with the Lord face to face (Joshua 3 to 6).

Gideon – What a wonderful visitation! He had an encounter with the Lord, and was equipped to destroy the Midianites. The cowardly, fearful man, hiding to thresh some wheat for food, became God's weapon to destroy the Midianites (Judges 6 through 7).

Stephen — A man filled with the Holy Spirit. He was being stoned to death for preaching the Word, yet in his dying moment, he saw Christ standing at the right hand of God. Stephen could pray the same prayer the Master prayed for His enemies, because He was enveloped with His presence (Acts 6 & 7).

* * * * * * *

Ruth, like the others mentioned, was also one who had been in the King's chamber. She knew who the God of Israel was. She had already tasted the worship of pagan gods, and knew the difference in having a relationship with the Living God. She knew the Lord God Jehovah as a covenant keeping God. Hence the reason she could affirm to Naomi,

"Your God shall be my God, The Lord do so to me also if ought but death part thee and me" (Ruth 1:16).

In other words, Ruth was saying to Naomi, "I will cling to the Lord as long as I live and keep this covenant I have made. If ever I break this promise, let God deal with me severely." From this point of view, I believe that Ruth had indeed a deep relationship with the Lord God of Israel.

Intimacy comes through prayer. Intimacy comes through praise. Intimacy comes through a personal encounter with the Holy Spirit. We must be hungry for more of the Lord before we can get intimate with Him.

We cannot enter into our prophetic destiny without an intimate relationship with the fulfiller of that prophecy. We are being called out to impact lives. It will never happen without His life being imbedded deeply within our lives.

Daughters of the King, intimacy with the King is not optional. If you have a hard time praying your way into His presence, please, begin to ask the Holy Spirit to draw you closer into the inner chamber of the King. Ask Him to wake you up at a certain time, and believe me, He will. It is a daily consecration. It is a daily renewal of clothing one's self with the Lord. It is not just a feeling, but a presence indescribable. It fills your entire being and you don't want to leave His presence. It is not a dream but a reality; for when He comes to fellowship with you, you know perfectly well He is there.

QUOTABLE QUOTES

"I have been driven many times to my knees by the overwhelming conviction that I had nowhere else to go. My own wisdom, and that of all about me, seemed insufficient for the day."

Abraham Lincoln (1809-1865)

[10]

ACCESS INTO THE INNER CHAMBER

(Touching The Heart of God And The Lives Of Men)

❖

"Now that we have what we have—Jesus, the great High Priest with ready access to God—let's not let it slip through our fingers. We don't have a priest who is out of touch with our reality. He's been through weakness and testing, experienced it all—all but the sin. So let's walk right up to Him and get what He is so ready to give. Take the mercy, accept the help" (Hebrews 4:14-16; Hebrews 10:19-20 – The Message).

We live in a fast track, fast paced world that nobody has time to do anything for anybody including God. We go through drive through in order to get whatever we want fast. We have fast lanes for fast drivers with passengers, and driving slowly or taking one's time to do whatever is necessary is deemed laziness. Many have easy lifestyles we think we do not need anything from God other than going to Church, and to enjoy our private lives.

We deal with God our Creator in the same manner. We don't have time to deal with human beings, and so God doesn't deserve the service of praying to often also. No wonder we have lots of "spiritual casualties" in the house of God — Lots of rebellion, unnecessary divorce, rampant lawlessness, lots of emotional problem, lots of marital infidelity, lots of juvenile delinquencies in the church, and the lists go on and on.

America's problem began when prayer was removed from the schools. Then the Bible followed, and then everything about Christ is now being contested. And now, the Nation that brought us the Bible, and has thrown Bibles out of schools, has now become a mission field, while religious education, church services are now booming in most African schools, and some parts of the world.

Africa is still thriving amidst all the wars, plagues, famine... because Christians in Africa know how to pray. Under normal circumstances and human reasoning, the people of Africa should not be in existence today. In the midst of wars, homicides, aids, and all the atrocities going on, there should be no survivals in that continent. Yet, Africa is still standing against all hope. Why? Christians in that land know how to pray.

We had a slogan for the Scripture Union I was a part of some years ago, which read "Pray until you die!" And we really meant it. We pray for everything – for health, for protection, for food supply, for financial breakthrough, and for everything. I mean everything. When you don't have health insurance and money to see the doctor, the only thing you need is a miracle. We prayed morning, afternoon, and all nights.

Prayer is the clutch on which I lean. And when I stumble, I fall right into the arms of Jesus.

"O GOD, Thou art my God; early will I seek Thee: my soul thirsteth for Thee, my flesh longeth for Thee in a dry and thirsty land, where no water is; to see Thy power and Thy glory, so as I have seen Thee in the sanctuary. Because Thy loving-kindness is better than life, my lips shall praise Thee. Thus will I bless Thee while I live: I will lift up my hands to Thy name. My soul shall be satisfied as with marrow and fatness; and my mouth shall praise Thee with joyful lips; when I remember Thee upon my bed, and meditate on Thee in the night watches. Because Thou hast been my help, therefore in the shadow of Thy wings will I rejoice. My soul followeth hard after Thee: Thy right hand upholdeth me" (Psalms 63:1-8).

So then, what is prayer? Prayer is an act of communing with God. It is a fervent request – to implore, to entreat, to move or to bring down. So to be prayerful means: To commune with God fervently, continuously, consistently, persistently, and effectively. To be devoted to prayer until something happens – till one is fused together with The Beloved. Friends, prayer ushers the child of God into the inner chamber of God for spiritual business.

EFFECTIVENESS OF PRAYER

My husband was dying. I did not want him to die. I knew God has been faithful in answering my prayers in the past. I have seen the dead raised, barren women becoming mothers, and countless miracles. The ministry He gave us moved in the miraculous. However, as I watched him lying in the couch at the Lawton's home, I knew something was snatching him away from my hand. I went inside the room and began calling him out of the dead silently.

"Geoffrey, come out from the dead. Geoffrey, come out from the dead." Something happened in the realm of the spirit. Then I heard Geoffrey call my name suddenly.
"What were you doing in the room over there?" He interrogated.
"I was praying for you. I want you to live, Darling." I said.
"Please, don't do that again. Leave me alone."
"No, I am praying you out of the dead," I said very frustrated. "You are not going anywhere."
"Yes, I know that, but please don't pray that prayer again," Geoffrey responded. "I am ready to go and be with the Lord. I don't want you to pray me out of the dead again."

I was very much disappointment. However, I knew my prayer was effective, but the recipient was not willing to stay here on earth. Geoffrey and his Heavenly Father had already closed up a deal well hidden from me. So a week later he passed to glory.

You see, when a believer prays fervently, something happens in the invisible. There is a shifting of events in the spiritual realm which affects the physical. So prayer should be part and parcel of every believer's life. Why? It is because all the Old and New Testaments saints prayed. Let's see few examples starting from our Lord.

- Jesus – God in the flesh prayed (Matthew 14:22-23; 26:39-44; Mark 6:46; 14:32-39; Luke 5:16; John 17).
- Abraham prayed (Genesis 20:17).
- Jacob prayed (Genesis 28:20-22; 32:9-12).
- Moses prayed (Numbers 11:2, 10-15; Numbers 21:7; Deuteronomy 9:20, 26-29)
- Hannah prayed (I Samuel 110-18, 26-28; 2:1-11).
- Samuel prayed (I Samuel 8:21).
- Elijah prayed (I Kings 18:36-46; James 5:17-18).
- Elisha prayed (2 King 6:16-18). David prayed (1 Chronicles 29: 10-19).
- Solomon prayed (2 Chronicles 6:12-42; 7:1-3).
- Hezekiah prayed (2 King 19:15-20; Isaiah 37:15-21).
- Esther prayed (Esther 3, 4).
- The Prophets prayed (2 Chronicles 32:20; Jeremiah 32:16-25; Daniel 6:10; 9:3-19; Jonah 2:1; 4:2).
- The Priests prayed (Ezra 19:1-15; 10:1, Nehemiah 1:4-11; 9:4-38).
- The Disciples prayed (Acts 1:24).
- The Early Church prayed (Acts 12:5-12; Acts 21:5).

All the saints prayed. And we must pray! (Luke 18:1-8; Ephesians 6:10-20; I Thessalonians 5:17)

You may still ask, 'Who then must pray'? Pastors or members, mature or immature, weak or strong believers must pray? Everybody must pray! No one is above prayers. Men must pray, women must pray, children must pray, and young people should even pray the more. Prayer is very important, and vital to our spiritual life—our victory over the flesh, over the enemy, and over every circumstance. Why? Because:

Ø PRAYER: A PRIVILEGE GIVEN TO MEN BY GOD

"Let us then approach the throne of grace with confidence, so that we may receive mercy and grace to help us in our time of need" (Hebrew 4:16).
"Draw nigh to God and He will draw nigh to you" (James 4:8 KJV). "Come near to God and He will come near to you" (James 4:8 NIV).

Jesus, through His death on the cross, paved the way back to God for every believer. The veil that separated us from God is removed. We can now call God, the Creator of the Heavens and the earth "Daddy, Abba Father" (Romans 8:16).

God has placed in the hands of every believer a privilege that unbelievers don't have. That is the privilege of having the Eternal God, the Mighty Creator, the All-Powerful, and the Great I AM as their Father – to communicate with Him in prayer concerning whatever need we may have.

Prayer is a special advantage given to every believer. It is your right to approach God, as a Father, in the name of His Son Jesus Christ. Prayer is a special benefit granted to every child of God to enjoy. Jesus said,

"Ask and it will be given to you; seek and you will find; knock and the door will be opened to you. For everyone who asks received; he who seeks finds; and to him who knocks, the door will be opened" (Matthew 7:7-8)

"And I will whatever you ask in My name, so that the Son may bring glory to the Father. You may ask Me for anything in My name, and I will do it" (John 14:13-14).

You are preferred above all of His creation, because you are His cherished daughter (possession). If you can't pray you are missing out on something special. God is waiting every moment to hear your voice. He leans on His heavenly balcony/porch each day waiting for your phone calls every minute. He enjoys you talking to Him.

Ø PRAYER: A LOVE AFFAIR BETWEEN CHRIST AND THE BELIEVER

"Take me away with you – let us hurry! Let the king bring me into his chambers. …. I am a rose of Sharon, a lily of the valleys. Like a lily among thorns, is my darling among the maidens. Like an apple tree among the trees of the forest is my lover among the young men. I delight to sit in his shade, and his fruit is sweet to my taste. He has taken me to His banqueting table and his banner over me is love. My lover spoke and said to me, 'Arise, my darling, my beautiful one and come with me. In the hiding places on the mountainside, show me your face, let me hear your voice; for your voice is sweet. …when I found the one my heart loves; I held him and would not let him go. Place me like a seal over your heart, like a seal on your arm; for love is as strong as death, its jealousy unyielding as the grave. It burns like blazing fire, like a mighty flame. Many waters cannot quench love; rivers cannot wash it away. If it were to give all the wealth of his house for love, it would be utterly scorned" (Song of Solomon 1:4, 2:1-5,10, 14; 3:4; 8:6-7).

"Be imitators of God, therefore, as dearly loved children and live a life of love, just as Christ loved us and gave Himself up for us as a fragrant offering and sacrifice to God. … Husbands, love your wives, just as Christ loved the Church, and gave Himself up for her to make her holy, cleansing her by the washing with water through the Word, and to present her to Himself as a radiant Church, without stain or wrinkle or any other blemish, but holy and blameless" (Ephesians 5:1-2, 25-27).

How many of you have ever fallen in love with someone? How much time did you or do you spend a day with your earthly lover? What about our eternal Lover – the Lover of your soul?

GOD'S LOVE

Everything about Him in regard to His relationship with us is out of true pure love for us. It is out of 'Agape' for you and me that He sat down, and drew the plan of salvation, in order for Him to unite with us and to recuperate that which was lost in Adam. The Scripture says,

"For God so loved the world that He gave His only Begotten Son ..." (John 3:16).
"God commended His Love towards us in that while we were yet sinners Christ died for us" (Roman 5:8).

This is the reason why He gave us this first commandment in Mathew 22:37 which states,

"Love the Lord your God with all your heart, with all your soul, and with all your mind" (Old Testament reference: Deuteronomy 6:5).

If we've really fallen in love with the Lord, with everything about us and in us, it won't be hard to be with Him every moment of our lives.

My two oldest sons just got married. Before they fell in love, I was their center of attraction. They called me night and day for everything and about everything; especially when they were not working. Now Mama is out of the picture. I can't believe they don't have time now for Mama even to answer some important questions I may need their help.

THE COVENANT RELATIONSHIP

The Song of Solomon is a magnificent song of a covenant love relationship between Christ and His Bride (the Church). God reached out His hand to you and me, and brought us into a covenant relationship between Christ and His Church – you and me. Love and Grace fused our hearts to His the moment you and I accepted His Son.

My husband's death is like a stab in my heart. I miss him so much because I loved him with all my heart. He was my friend, brother and everything to me. This is what true love is. Excluding all other lovers, the love of your Lord, can never ever fail you one minute. He doesn't even die. He is forever with us.

Every believer is like tiny flowers planted on the side of a mountain or an open field facing life's hurricanes and tornadoes. Without prayer we become like weaklings and dummies before the enemy. But through prayer, God's Spirit fills us with power to live as He desires. Through prayer, we find satisfaction in the sound of The Name that quenches the deepest thirst in our soul. Through prayer, we find peace and joy even in the darkest moments of our lives.

Through prayer, His grace helps us to thrive like roses among the thorns of our mistakes, failures, weaknesses and even betrayals. Through prayer and intercession, we can shed tears of compassion for even those who hurt us. Through prayer, we move His heart to mercy, to forgiveness of sins, to the restoration of nations, and His hands act on our behalf also. Through prayer, we find the answer to our every need in Christ's name.

Through prayer, we gain strength to fight until victory is won in any given circumstance. God's love draws our roots deep down into the soil of Who He is, like the palm trees in Africa, which always stand tall no matter what, so that we can stand any storm, and be fruitful in all dimensions with the new life that He has given to us.

Remember, prayer is a command. Jesus said, "…Men ought always to pray and not to faint" (Luke 18:1). How deep is your love for God? Deep love for God will ultimately result in total obedience to His commands.

> Jesus says again, "If you love Me, you will obey what I command. Whoever has My commands and obey them, he is the one who loves Me. He who loves Me, will be loved by My Father, and I too will love Him, and show Myself to him" (John 14:15, 21).

"Pray without ceasing" (I Thessalonians 5:17).

"I exhort therefore, that, first of all, supplications, prayers, intercessions, and giving of thanks, be made for all men; for kings, and for all that are in authority; that we may lead a quiet and peaceable life in all godliness and honesty. For this is good and acceptable in the sight of God our Savior; Who will have all men to be saved, and to come into the knowledge of the truth" (I Timothy 2:1-4).

Ø PRAYER: AN INTIMATE RELATIONSHIP BETWEEN CHRIST AND HIS CHURCH

"As the Father has loved Me, so have I loved you. Now remain in my love" (John 15: 9).

True love results ultimately in deep intimacy. True intimacy starts when two hearts blend together in true pure love one for the other. If we really evaluate our love for the Lord, and begin to engage in true love conversation with Him, we become very intimate with Him. Jesus compared our intimacy with Him with the vine and its branches. He says,

> "Remain (be intimate, be rooted firmly, fixed, deep-seated, embedded, entrenched, ingrained) in Me and I will remain in you. ...I am the vine; you are the branches ..." (John 15:4, 5 – emphasis mine).

There are so many things in our vineyards that are fighting against our prayer life — intimacy with the Lord. They are very promising to us, and we tend to sacrifice the precious moment we can spend with God.

- **Our jobs and careers say**: 'Give me more overtime and you will be financially fit, you will really have everything you need in this life.' Is this really true? More money without an intimate relationship with the Giver is vanity. And it becomes an obsession.
- **Our family says**: 'Let us have more fun together, make us your top priority and you will be happy— the ball games, the vacations and all the fun.' They pressure us with the notion that the more you have much of these, the better your life is. Is it true? Not obvious! The health of your family lies in the person and the presence of our Lord Jesus Christ.

- **The world around us says**: 'Plug in into more riches or pleasure and you will find yourself. The more money you have, the happier you will be.' To find self, you must find God and cultivate an intimate relationship with Him. In reality, more money doesn't bring happiness. *"Happiness is to know the Savior, living a life within His favor, having a change in my behavior, happiness is the Lord. Real joy is mine no matter if tear drop cries. I've found the secret; it is Jesus in my heart. Happiness is a new creation, Jesus and me in close relation, having a part in His salvation, happiness is the Lord,"* reads the old song.
- **Religious activities**: Even religious activities can take our prayer life away. Religious activities can snatch away a personal intimate relationship with the Lord. You see, religion without a relationship with the Author of life is meaningless and vague. I believe Christ did not come to establish a religion, but a relationship with the Father—that which was lost through Adam restored. Our number one priority in life as Christians is, loving the Lord with all our hearts, with all our minds, and with all our strength (Deuteronomy 6:5-8).

Jesus, the True Lover of our souls is the only True Vine we need to attach ourselves to. He says, *"I am the true vine, you are the branches" (John 15:5).* There are many wild vines all around us trying to snatch away our time with the Lord. All of these vines, even though they are good, cannot compete with the fulfillment that comes as a result of an intimate relationship with the Lord. Please fall in love with Jesus because:

- True lovers communicate with each other.
- True lovers can't help being away from each.
- True lovers stay on the line forever talking about stuff; even when unnecessary. But with God, every bit of what you say is very important to Him.
- True lovers are fond of each other. They go crazily wild for each other. Our Lord Jesus is crazily in love with us. Are you?
- True love affair is a lifetime commitment. It's an agreement signed never to depart from each other no matter how the going might be (Romans 8:28-39). I have signed a lifetime agreement with the Lover of my soul.
- True lovers are wired together. It is hard to separate them. Everywhere, they go together. It is kind of like the old song about the Bible entitled 'I have a wonderful treasure'.

True joy, true satisfaction, immense strength, and a better understanding of rightful place in this world is only found in the life of an individual who is very intimate with God.

Ø PRAYER: FRIENDSHIP WITH GOD

"Greater love has no one than this that he lay down his life for his friends. You are my friends if you do what I command you. I no longer call you servants, because a servant does not know his master's business. Instead I call you friends, for everything that I learned of my Father I have made known to you." (John 15:13-15)

How did Abraham become the friend of God? How did he hear the call to go to a land he did not know, and how did he survive all the turmoil in his life? As said earlier, I believe Abraham was a man of prayer. And because prayer is a two-way communication, he talked to God and God spoke to him. Abraham was a prayer warrior, an intercessor, and a prophet. We read in the Bible, "And Abraham said to the Lord. ... And God said to Abraham." The Lord could not help but tell Abraham what He was going to do to Sodom and Gomorrah because he was His Friend! This is what is called True Friendship, and it comes as a result of prayer (Isaiah 41:8).

How did David become a man after God's own heart? The Book of Psalms explains it clearly. He loved to talk to and with God. No wonder the Psalms are filled with prophetic utterances concerning the Messiah. In Psalm 55: 17, King David sang, *"Listen to my prayer, Oh God, do not ignore my plea; hear me and answer me. ...Evening, morning and noon I cry out to you in distress, and he hears my voice."* David prayed almost all day. He was attached to the Lord.

> "Jesus said to His disciples, "I no longer call you servants, because a servant does not know his master's business. Instead, I call you friends, for everything that I learned from my Father I have made known to you" (John 15:14-15).

Why did Jesus call the disciples His friends? It is because they were very close to Him. They ate together. They traveled together. They ministered together. They communed with Him, and He communed with them. All the times they made mistakes or betrayed Him, were when He wasn't close to them.

With these three examples, we've seen a precedence of God calling some individuals His friends. Why? True friends hang out together for hours without being tired. True friends talk about stuff. True friends do things together. True friends share secrets among themselves. True friends confide in each other. The Bible came to us as a result of an intimate relationship people had with God. The Bible says:

"All secret things belong to God" (Deuteronomy 29:29).
"The secret of the Lord is with them that fear Him, and He will show them His covenant" (Psalm 25:11).
"Surely the Sovereign Lord does nothing without revealing his plan to his servants the prophet" (Amos 3:7).

I do not know what I would have done without prayer. With all the stuff I have been through, talking to God, and listening to His instruction, is what has kept me standing. I talk to Him anytime, anywhere, and everywhere. And He also communes with me.

This old hymn, labeled anonymous, and may have been rearranged by J. C. Ludgate, explains it much better. It reads,

A Friend of Jesus, oh, what bliss
That one so weak as I
Should ever have a Friend like this,
To lead me to the sky
A Friend when other friendship cease,
A Friend when others fail
A Friend who gives me joy and peace,
A Friend who will prevail
A Friend who leads me in the dark,
A Friend who knows the way
A Friend to steer my weak, frail back,
A Friend my debts to pay
A Friend when sickness lays me low,
A Friend when death draws near

A Friend as through the vale I go,
A Friend to help and cheer
A Friend when life's voyage is over,
A Friend when death is past
A Friend to greet on Heaven's shore,
A Friend when home at last
Friendship with Jesus, Fellowship divine
Oh what blessed sweet communion.
Jesus is a Friend of mine

(Taken from Hymns of Glorious Praise No 338 – By Gospel Publishing House – Springfield, Missouri)

Ø PRAYER: FELLOWSHIPING WITH THE HOLY SPIRIT OF GOD

"May the grace of our Lord Jesus Christ, and the love of the God, and the **fellowship** of the Holy Spirit be with you" (II Corinthians 13:14).

"If you have any encouragement from being united with Christ, if any comfort from his love, if any **fellowship** with the Spirit ..." (Philippians 2:1).

"In the same way, the Spirit helps us in our weakness. We do not know what we ought to pray for, but the Spirit Himself intercedes for us with groans what words cannot express. And He who searches our hearts, knows the mind of the Spirit, because the Spirit intercedes for the saints in accordance with God's will" (Romans 8:26-27).

Fellowship: Someone said: "Fellowship is two fellows in a ship." I like that. We are all in the same boat with Jesus sailing together to Heaven. Any of us who tries to jump overboard without Him will surely drown. Any who tries and oars his/her life's boat without Him, the wind will teach you a lesson of total dependency on Him through prayer.

When we pray, we deepen our relationship not only with God the Father and Jesus Christ our Bridegroom; we also deepen our relationship, our fellowship (communion) with the Holy Spirit. The Holy Spirit is the One who has come to walk alongside with us in this Christian journey. Although we may not know what we should pray for, however when we make an effort to pray, the Holy Spirit enables us to touch the heart of God. We then come in agreement with Him concerning what the will of God should be. To affirm this, we read again,

"... The Spirit helps us in our weakness. We do not know what we ought to pray for, but the Sprit Himself intercedes for us with groans that words cannot express. And He who searches our heart, knows the mind of the Spirit, because the Spirit intercedes for the saints in accordance with God's will" (Rom 8:26-27).

Many Christians think that the Holy Spirit came only to make us witnesses of Christ. Yes, it is true but when you develop this fellowship with Him, He will enable you to pray more. He will renew your spiritual life. He will strengthen you in your weakness. He will illumine your spirit mind to understand deep spiritual things. He will give you a discerning heart. He will empower you to overcome sin. He will guide you into all truth, and He will give you courage and boldness to share your faith with others. He will enable you to handle life's situations and challenges with courage. He will definitely empower us to even die for Him. That is what a witness is: a martyr.

Every believer in Christ needs to deepen their relationship with the Holy Spirit. We need to start communing with the Holy Spirit each moment as we pray in the prayer language He has given us. The devil does not even understand it. Even if you don't know how to pray; this will be a great opportunity for the Holy Spirit to help you go deeper in your prayer life. Please, ask Him to fill you with His Holy Spirit.

Ø PRAYER: A SPIRITUAL BUSINESS AGREEMENT WITH THE ALMIGHTY

"I will give you the keys of the kingdom of heaven; whatever you bind on earth will be bound in heaven, and whatever you loose on earth will be loosed in heaven" (Matthew 16:19).

"I tell you the truth, whatever you bind on earth will be bound in heaven, and whatever you loose on earth will be loosed in heaven. Again, I tell you if two of you on earth agree about anything you ask for, it will be done for you by My Father in heaven. For where two or three come together in My name, there am I with you" (Matthew 18:18-20).

The moment you and I accepted the Lord, we signed a contract, an agreement with the Almighty God – a contract to be partners in agreeing with Him in accomplishing great things on earth. This agreement confirms the prayer Jesus taught the disciples.

"He (Jesus) said to them, "When you pray, say: "Our Father in heaven, hallowed be Your name, Your kingdom come. May Your will be done on earth as it is in heaven. Give us each day our daily bread. Forgive us our debts, as we also have forgiven our debtors. And lead us not into temptation but deliver us from the evil one. For Thine is the kingdom, and the power and the glory for ever, (Amen)" (Matthew 6:9-15; Also Luke 11:1-4).

Let us look at a few or partial list of the agreement we signed with the Lord.

- **To pray and destroy the kingdom of darkness**. "I have given you authority to trample on snakes and scorpions and to overcome all the power of the enemy; nothing will harm you." "And these signs will accompany those who believe. In My name they will drive out demons; ...." (Luke 10:19; Mark 16:17-19).

- **To pray His kingdom down on earth.** "When you pray ... Thy Kingdom come ... Thy will be done on earth as it is done in Heaven" (Luke 11:2b).
- **To pray that His will be done on earth as it is done in heaven** "Whatsoever you bind on earth ..." Matthew 6:9).
- **To pray for the salvation of others.** We are soul watchers. "Son of man, I have made you a watchman for the house of Israel; so hear the word I speak and give them warning from Me. When I say to the wicked, 'You will surely die,' and you do not warn him or speak out to dissuade him from his evil ways in order to save his life, that wicked man will die in his sin, and I will hold you accountable for his blood. But if you do warn the wicked man and he does not turn from his wickedness, or from his evil ways, he will die for his sin, but you will have saved yourself" (Ezekiel 3:17-18). Read also First Timothy 2:1-4.
- **To pray for harvesters or laborers.** "Jesus went through all the towns and villages, teaching in their synagogues, preaching the good news of the kingdom and healing every disease and sickness. When He saw the crowds, He had compassion on them, because they were harassed and helpless, like sheep without a shepherd. Then He said to His disciples, '*The harvest is plentiful but the workers are few. Ask the Lord of the harvest, therefore, to send out worker into His harvest field*'" (Matthew 9:37 – emphasis mine). Read also Luke 10:1-2.
- **To be like Jesus.** "And we, who with unveiled faces all reflect the Lord's glory, are being transformed into His likeness with ever-increasing glory, which comes from the Lord, who is the Spirit" (2 Corinthians 3:18). Also Ephesians 1:3-14; 4:17-24.

- **To persevere in our relationship with Him without turning aside.** "Be thou faithful unto the end, and I will give unto thee the crown of life" (Revelation 3:10). "...He who stands firm to the end shall be saved" (Matthew 24:13).
- **To pray for proper God-fearing human governing in nations.** "I urge, then, first of all, that request, prayers, intercession and thanksgiving be made for everyone—for kings and all those in authority, that we may live peaceful and quiet lives in all godliness and holiness. This is good, and pleases God our Savior, who wants all men to be saved and to come to the knowledge of the truth; for there is one God and one Mediator between God and men, the Man Christ Jesus, who gave Himself as a ransom for all men—the testimony given in its proper time" (I Timothy 2:1-4).
- **To pray for our spiritual leaders.** "Devote yourselves to prayer, being watchful and thankful. And pray for us, too, that God may open a door for our message, so that we may proclaim the mystery of Christ, for which I am in chains. Pray that I may proclaim it clearly, as I should" (Colossians 4:2-4). "Brothers, pray for us" (1 Thessalonians 5:25).
- **To support one another in the faith.** "Carry each other's burdens, and in this way you will fulfill the law of Christ" (Galatians 6:2).

Why such an agreement? Is God not sufficient in Himself to do all things by Himself? What does He need me for? Yes, God is All-powerful, however He created you and I to be His ambassadors on earth to represent the Kingdom. Every decision an ambassador makes must be in line with what His government has already established. We collaborate with Him in establishing His Kingdom on Earth.

Why did Jesus ask the people to loose Lazarus after He has called Him forth from the dead? He could have just completed the work without any human effort, but he wanted them to participate in His finished work. He also wanted to boost up their faith in Him as the Messiah.

Why did Jesus give the bread to the disciples to distribute to the people? He could have rained down bread from Heaven. Why did Jesus send the disciples to loose the donkey for His triumphant entry into Jerusalem? He knew where the donkey was, and could have just walked to it and ridden through the city without their help, or He could have called forth the donkey, and it would have obeyed. You see, Christ wanted His disciples to participate in the fulfillment of prophecy. God requires us to do what we can, not what we cannot do. He simply told King Solomon: "If my people who are called by My Name shall humble themselves...and pray... Then I will forgive, and heal their land" (II Chronicles 7:14).

He told the disciples, "If two shall agree concerning anything... I will do it" (Matthew 18:19). In other words, God is saying, "If you do your part, you will see the end result of My faithfulness – I will complete My part, because it is already settled in Heaven. If you pray, I will act because I am a covenant keeping God!"

EVERY NATION'S DESTINY

The country of Togo was going through the worse political instability I had ever seen. It started from 1986 terrorist activities, and escalated into something else. However, from 1986 to 1992, the turmoil increased and many died. We knew that Togo was at the verge of civil war and homicides. Before all these political problems began, the Lord gave me a vision which startled me. 'I saw a mighty angel standing on the continent of Africa holding a huge sword. When he lifted up the sword, a boisterous wind began to blow; and it swept through the whole continent. Then blood began to flow'. This dream was given to me in 1981. The Lord spoke to me and said, "This is the wind of lawlessness and democracy. It will sweep through the whole land, and cause a lot of havoc. ...... "

"Is democracy not good?" I asked the Lord.

The Lord said, "Monica, what is the definition of democracy? Is it not government of the people, by the people and for the people?"

"Yes Lord," I responded.

"There is no mention of My name. My Kingdom is not democracy. My kingdom is Theocracy. This World is Mine. I AM the Supreme Commander and the Sovereign Governor of this World. No one chose Me to be the Governor of this universe. No one can vote Me in to power. I AM the All-Powerful! I rule because I AM Who I AM! Democracy breeds lawlessness, and opposes anything that is Godly. I have given men free-will; the ability to make right choices, and to obey My Word. Whatever they do with their free-will, will affect their own destiny, and not Mine; and they will account for every choice; for every manner of life they lived; whether good or bad. However, I want to tell you that the destiny of each nation depends on My children. The destiny of Togo is in your hands. Whatever you want this nation to be, so will it be. Whatever you decree shall be."

I actually forgot about the dream, but when the problems escalated, the Holy Spirit reminded Geoffrey and me of the dream. We gathered our family together and began praying to cancel the spirit of war. The church joined us, and together, we interceded for Africa, but especially for Togo. The Lord heard our prayers. Unbelievably, Togo is still standing, although it's been through a lot of instabilities, and is still shaky. But the prayer of the righteous is still powerful.

Church, we surely have a business agreement with God concerning anything we desire for His glory.

Ø PRAYER: THE SPIRITUAL BREATH OF THE CHRISTIAN

"Then Jesus told his disciples a parable to show them that they should always pray and not give up" (Luke 18:1).
"Why are you sleeping?" He asked them. "Get up and pray so that you will not fall into temptation. The Spirit indeed is willing, but the flesh is weak" (Luke 22:46).
"Pray without ceasing" (I Thessalonians 5:17).

If a Christian ceases to pray he/she suffocates spiritually, and will suffer from spiritual shortness of breath. God does not put His children on artificial inhaler or respirator for spiritual growth. There is no such thing in His warehouse. His divine power is able to infuse new strength, new life into any of His children, who has learned to pray without ceasing. It is called the study of "Kneeology." It is not taught in any school. It is an individual's daily spiritual training on his or her knees for everything. You start praying and the miracle begins.

Do you know the kind of sicknesses prayerless Christians suffer from?

- They become weak and ineffective because they develop spiritual anemia. (Psalms 73; Psalms 119:81-83; 124)
- They are not able to stand tall in face of any spiritual exercise because they have spiritual fibromyagia or arthritis. (Psalm 119:105-112; Psalms 121)

- They are easily frustrated and tired because they suffer from spiritual chronic fatigue. But "They that wait upon the Lord shall renew their strength. They shall run and not be weary; they shall walk and not faint" (Isaiah 40:31). Please read Psalms 23 also.
- The Christian life becomes a burden not a pleasure because they suffer from Spiritual paralysis. (Psalm 119:116-117; Psalms 125)
- They can't stand the enemy because they suffer from Spiritual panic and anxiety attacks. (Psalms 27; Psalms 91)

Ø PRAYER: A RENDEZVOUS WITH HIS MAJESTY

Most churches have fixed time for church services or prayer meetings. That is very necessary. However, many fail to start on time because the pastor or whoever is in charge wants to wait for late-comers.

My late husband Geoffrey was a man who respected time very much. Before this time, he would wait for at least ten to fifteen minutes to make room for late-comers before starting the services. He wasn't like that in the past, but an incident changed his life forever. He had a dream one day that he went to the church as usual to teach Bible study. There was no one at the church upon his arrival. It was almost thirty minutes to seven in the evening. As he knelt down to pray, he heard the footsteps of someone entering the room. He didn't get up. He already knew it was almost time for service, and knew in his heart that maybe that could be a member, walking down the aisle to take a seat. But something unusual happened. The steps got louder and closer to where he was and faded away.

Interesting? Yes of course! But that wasn't the end. The person sat next to him. That didn't disturb him either. He continued to pray. At ten till, he got up to prepare himself to teach. To his amazement, the guest sitting next to him was the Lord. He did not know what to do. He bent over to welcome Him. Then he looked at his time, and it was seven o'clock on the dot. He glanced back at the congregation. There were only ten people sitting in the pew praying silently.

As usual, he wanted to wait for ten more minutes. At that time, the Lord spoke to him and said: 'You made a rendezvous with me at 7 o'clock. I respect My time, and so I was here early to wait for you. It is seven. Let's start our meeting..."

He dragged his feet for a while, trying to while away the time before beginning the Bible studies. More people were now entering. Just at that time, he sensed something was wrong. There was an unusual feeling in his spirit. He couldn't figure out what it was. Worst of all, the anointing and the presence of the Lord that he felt at the onset of his entrance into the church wasn't there. Then he remembered that the Lord was sitting behind him. He turned around to ask Him what the problem was. To his amazement, He was gone. The Lord had left. Wow!

What a dream! He woke up sobbing so loud. A week after he had a similar dream. This time the Lord spoke to him directly and said: *"My people do not take the time they fix to meet with Me very serious. Many Christians do not get what they've been praying for because they miss the timing. I am always there when I am invited. If earthly leaders respect their rendezvous, what about Me? I also work with time. ..."*

From that moment, he decided to respect the time allotted for church services, and was known to be an 'on-time pastor'.

While studying the book of Numbers, my eyes caught these verses, which I believe, confirms this dream. In my book "God Still Speaks", I talked about the encounter I had with the Lord, where He reprimanded me for not obeying His command to leave Togo in 1995 to come to the United States precisely. I dragged my feet for a long time till disaster hit me very hard. I played with His timing, and I am still facing the consequences for not accepting the call at that specific time. God respects His time. It may not be what I want, but when I have negotiated that time with Him, I am obliged to respect it.

> "On the day the tabernacle, the Tent of the Testimony, was set up, the cloud covered it. From evening till morning the cloud above the tabernacle looked like fire. ...*Whenever the cloud lifted from above the Tent, the Israelites set out; wherever the cloud settled, the Israelites encamped.* At the Lord's command, the Israelites set out, and at his command they encamped. As long as the cloud stayed over the tabernacle, they remained in camp. When the cloud remained a long time, the Israelites obeyed the Lord's order and did not set out. Sometimes the cloud was over the tabernacle only a few days; at the Lord's command they would encamp, and at the Lord's command, they would set out. Sometimes the cloud stayed from evening till morning, and when it lifted in the morning. They set out. Whether the cloud stayed over the tabernacle for two days or a month, or a year, the Israelites would remain in camp and not set out; but when it lifted, they would set out. *At the Lord's command they encamped, and at the Lord's command they set out. They obeyed the Lord's order, in accordance with his command through Moses"* (Numbers 11:15-23 – emphasis mine).

A RENDEZVOUS WITH HIS MAJESTY

What is a rendezvous? A rendezvous is an arranged meeting, to meet at a specific place and time for an important affair, or to discuss an important issue.

Every born again believer has a rendezvous, a special meeting with His Majesty, the King of the universe in the form of prayer and intercession. Most important of all, our prayer time, is the fixed time we have vowed, or set with the Holy Spirit to pray. He always comes at the right time to commune with us. Moreover, believe me; angels are dispatched at that specific time to take our prayers to the throne room of God, and to bring back the answers right away. Believe this or not, this is a revelation I had from the Lord.

In my walk with the Lord for these 44 years, I have come to understand that despite the fact that God loves me very much does not mean I should take His Greatness and His Majesty for granted. He has taught me these three important truths:

I – The Opportunity: The opportunity given to you and me to meet with the King of kings must be cherished. It cost Him the death of His Son to give us that special access. This day of full purchase of our redemption, marked the whole universe. God veiled Himself away from His Only Son. There was an earthquake. Rocks were split in pieces, and the Temple curtain was ripped in two. Tombs were opened, and Old Testament saints walked out of their tombs, and appeared to many. Darkness fell for three good hours; while the sun refused to shine. I believe this was the day Heaven stood still, and earth trembled. Does this mean something to God? Obviously! (Matthew 27:50-54; Luke 23:44-49).

II – The Timing: The time set for the meeting must be respected, because God also works with time. I know God works with time because His Word tells me so. Every prophecy we read in this Holy Book has God's timepiece attached to it. The deluge came at God's appointed time. Isaac was born at the appointed time. Joseph went to Egypt to become the savior of his people at God's appointed time. The hole, the slavery, and the prison were all in the sovereign plan of God for Joseph.

Moses was born, and became the deliverer at God's appointed time; at the set time given to Abraham before Joseph and Moses were ever conceived – 430years, from the time of Joseph's entrance into Egypt to the time of their deliverance. The set time given to the Prophet Jeremiah concerning the return of the Jews to rebuild the Temple to the time of the Messiah was fulfilled to the letter. Jesus came in to the world's scene at the set time. Oh brethren, we can go on and on. God does not play with His timing, because He is True, Just, and Faithful!

III - His Presence must be honored. The prophets proclaimed, "God is in this holy temple, let all the earth keep silent before Him." (Habakkuk 2:20; Zechariah 2:13)

What do you think will happen if the President of France had you on his calendar for a set meeting at 6p.m., and you showed up at 7p.m.? How do you think he would feel if you kept on postponing his set date and time? What do you think you will do in the presence of the president of the United States? Will you come in with your starbuck coffee, dressed shabbily, when it is in your power to dress right? Why do people dress right – in their best for special outings, family reunions, and business meetings, church dinners in hotels, and yet do the contrary when it comes to the house of God. I hope you understand that when God had blessed someone with the material, he or she must use it for His glory. But when you do not have it, God sees the depth of your heart. Be in your best for His glory and praise.

Will you enter in to the oval room talking on your cellphone with another person, yelling, and giggling, while Mr.

President sits looking at you? Or you will enter into his presence with respect and awe?

I walked in to the office of a chiropractor and sat on one of the chairs provided for patients, waiting for my turn. A sign on the wall in caps caught my attention. It reads: "IN CONSIDERATION OF OTHERS BEING TREATED, PLEASE TURN OFF ALL CELL PHONES, AND ENTER ROOM QUIETLY. YOUR COOPERATION IS VERY MUCH APPRECIATED."

Isn't that cute? Do you think people obey that particular instruction? Absolutely! I turned off mine even before I walked through the door. What if Christians learned to shut off cell phones before entering into the presence of the King of kings? I hope there could be a sign at the entrance of every sanctuary to read: "IN CONSIDERATION OF THE PRESENCE OF THE KING OF THE UNIVERSE, AND OF OTHERS SEEKING FOR ANSWERS FROM HIM, PLEASE TURN OFF ALL CELL PHONES, AND ENTER ROOM QUIETLY. TODAY MAY BE THE DAY FOR YOUR MIRACLE. YOUR COOPERATION IS VERY MUCH APPRECIATED. ANGELS ALREADY ON BOARD AND THE SPIRIT IS ALREADY MOVING HERE! THANKS!"

A lot of Christians in our 'civilized' world today do not respect the presence of the Lord. I am as guilty as anyone of you. We talk about grace and love, yet we have forgotten that true love will respect the privileges given without going over board. Grace does not give us the right to be disrespectful either.

True love and respect for someone places you in the position to honor the person, his or her time, and the opportunity set before you. Grace does not cancel the Majesty and holiness of God. It does not annul the respect and honor due to the Creator of the universe. The grace of God is rather giving to every believer to equip us to do the right thing (Titus 2:11-14).

THE IMPORTANCE OF PRAYER

Being prayerful is not automatic. Intimacy with God does not come easy. It is hard work but pleasant. Something must be done! One must desire to pray. Moreover, prayer is not optional. Prayer is a must! It is a command. And so first of all, we must consider these few steps.

1) **See Prayer see it as a need.** It is not an option. It is a need. Jesus said, "Pray". It is a must have. "Jesus told his disciples a parable to show them that they should always pray and not give up." (Luke 18:1).

"Pray continually" (1 Thessalonians 5:17).

2) **Be hungry for it (Have a strong desire).** "As the deer pants for streams of water, so my soul pants for you, O God. My soul thirsts for God for the living God. When can I go and meet God?" (Psalm 42:1-2) Crave for it. Don't settle for something less. If you get hungry or crave for something, you eat it. Let it be a driving force that will draw you closer to God.

3) **Work at it.** Cultivate the habit to pray. Put all your effort into it like blind Bartemaeus (Luke 18:35-43). Whether it is in the quietness of your room or in the middle of a noisy-busy area, driving your car to work or to buy groceries, God wants to commune with us. We can cry out, "Thou Son of David, have mercy on me." We can do it again and again. Jesus will stop by you.

4) **Build up a 'Can't live without it' mentality.** (Psalms 62:1) If you know you can't live without something, you find ways and means to get it or die. Your life and mine hang on prayer. It is the thread on which your soul hangs. If you do

not strengthen the cord it will break! Someone wrote, "Life is precious, handle it with prayer." Crave for it, and get it.
  5) **Let it be your passion.** Be persistent. Call out to Him again and again like the Syrophoenician woman, who persistently begged Jesus until she received the answer to her prayer. (Matthew 15:21-28)

THE LONGINGS OF THE HUMAN SOUL

"I slept but me heart was awake. Listen! My lover is knocking: Open to me, my sister, my darling, my dove, my flawless one. "My head is drenched with dew, my hair with the dampness of the night" I have taken off my robe—must I put it on again? I have washed my feet—must I soil them again? My lover thrust his hand through the latch-opening; my heart began to pound for him. I arose to open for my lover, and my hands dripped with myrrh, on the handles of the lock. I opened for my lover, but my lover had left, he was gone. My heart sank at his departure. I looked for him but did not find him. I called him but he did not answer. The watchmen found me as they made their rounds in the city. They beat me, they bruised me; they took away my cloak, those watchmen of the walls! O daughters of Jerusalem, I charge you—if you find my lover, what will you tell him? Tell him I am faint of love." (Song of Songs 5:2-8)

Each human heart yearns to have intimacy with his or her Creator. It cries for affection. It seeks for fellowship; and most important of all, it also desires to feel the presence of the One who created and fashioned him or her according to His image. However, life's turmoil, life's businesses tend to block our path to the intimacy we yearn for. Oftentimes, Christ, the Lover of our souls, stands behind the door of our lives, knocking and knocking, turning on and twisting the door latchet just to be asked to come in, in order to satisfy the longings in our souls. Yet we sometimes adamantly close our ears to the sound of His voice. His ardent desire is to be with us. We are His Beloved, and He is the Sweet Lover.

In the Scripture we read earlier, she, the beloved, hears the knock of the Lover on her door. She hears His voice calling her into intimacy, but she wanted to sleep. Although her body was sleeping, her heart was wide awake, because her soul was longing for intimacy. She saw His hand turning the door knob, *"My Lover thrust His hand through the latch-opening"* but she did not yield to His call. She did not want to get up. Her sleep was too sweet for her. It was not easy for her to leave the comfort of her bed. Her busyness, her own personal time to herself, was much valuable to her than the visit of Her Sweet Lover. Her agenda was more important than His presence. But you know what? True love will never rest until it finds its Lover.

Is this familiar to you? Have you ever turned down the wooing of the Spirit? Have you ever woken up in the middle of the night wondering why you couldn't go back to sleep? O how I want to sleep during those times! How many times has He knocked on your heart's door just to come in and use you to touch other lives in the quietness of your own room through prayer, but you wouldn't budge, because you are too tired to get up and commune with Him? Ponder on these, daughter of the King.

Now, when she finally opened the door, He was gone. He waited and waited, and finally left. *"I arose to open for my Lover, but my Lover had left; he was gone."* You see, the Lover came to the door just to tell her how beautiful she was. We are His bride. We are very precious and very unique to Him. He admires us and He desires us. 'All He wants is you, no one else will do' is the old song we've ceased singing, but it tells the very story of the Lover of our souls.

He always comes with a gift—the oil of His presence to soothe every pain, and to heal all our ills. He wants to anoint us with fresh oil—the oil of myrrh He left on the handles of the lock. He is waiting to give you and me a fresh start (verses 4-5).

King David understood the importance of being anointed with fresh oil in the Psalms he wrote.

"...You anoint my head with oil; my cup overflows. Surely goodness and love will follow me all the days of my life, and I will dwell in the house of the Lord forever" (Psalms 23:5-6).

He knew that the desire to be in the house of the Lord, and the overshadowing of His love and goodness was the direct result of the anointing that comes with His presence in his life. Your life will always overflow with divine favor when He comes in. Corrie ten Boom wrote, "Don't pray when you feel like it. Have an appointment with the Lord and keep it. A man is powerful on his knees."

Christ, our Beloved, is calling us away from the trivial things of life that obstruct our relationship with Him, so we might enjoy a deeper intimacy with Him. He wants to impregnate us with His presence to impact our society like the Apostles. Are we going to respond?

QUOTABLE QUOTES

"He belongs to you, but more than that, He longs to be in you, living and ruling in you as the head lives and rules in the body. He wants His breath to be in your breath, His heart in your heart, and His soul in your soul, so that you may indeed "Glorify God and bear Him in your body, that the life of Jesus may be made manifest in you."

Jean Eudes (1601-1680)

[11]

WOMEN WHO HAVE STRIPPED OFF SELF
(Total Surrender)

❖

"Catch for us the foxes, the little foxes that ruin the vineyards that are in bloom" (S.S 2:15).

"Those who live according to the sinful nature have their minds set on what that nature desires; but those who live in accordance with the Spirit have their minds set on what the Spirit desires. The mind of sinful man is death, but the mind controlled by the Spirit is life and peace; the sinful man is hostile to God. It does not submit to God's law, nor can it do so. Those controlled by the sinful nature cannot please God" (Romans 8:5-8).

It takes a willing vessel, one who is hungry enough to grab the feet of Christ, to reach out into a higher realm, and be ready to be used of God. The secret to this anointing is found in total surrender. Total surrender comes when we are willing to fall down in prayer, asking the Holy Spirit to break us, to melt us and to mold us into what He desires.

The anointing comes through brokenness. It is not a one-time event; it is a continual revelation of what God requires from us. It is a daily dying of one's self. It is yielding, repenting, consecrating, and dedicating one's self. It is a daily confession, purification or cleansing of one's self from all unwanted bits and pieces in our lives. It is a daily training, and the living of a life that is well pleasing to the Lord. The overcoming life is a daily walk with the risen Lord. It is not a one day done deal.

These end-time vessels are climbing up higher into a place of honor before God, and favor before men. You see, the Lord wants to use everybody, but He also requires that these vessels be used willingly and be cleansed from all hindrances and impurities.

> "But in a great house there are not only vessels of gold and of silver, but also of wood and of earth; and some to honor, and some to dishonor. If a man (woman) therefore purge himself from these, he shall be a vessel unto honor, sanctified, and meet for the master's use, and prepared unto every good work" (II Timothy 2:20-21).

Having been through the fire, these end-time vessels are unburnable. Nothing shakes their faith. They've been toughened. They have been refined. All the dross of past sins and evil behavior have been healed and taken away.

Having been through the waters, they have been purified and cleansed from the old life. They are transformed. They walk in the fear and awesomeness of God's holiness, having a fervent desire to please the Lord. They can say without a shadow of a doubt before everyone, "If any one be in Christ, he (she) is new" (2 Corinthians 5:17 emphasis mine). This verse is a powerful proclamation if it is lived!

As a result of their intimate relationship with the King, they have been transformed. They have put on Christ. Their spiritual eyes are opened to a deeper revelation of who their Heavenly Father is, and who they really are. As a result of their encounter with the Lord, self is being stripped away.

The price of sin has been paid already. The Holy Spirit is already given. The only hindrance to revival is SELF. Self drags churches to sail endlessly on lifeless cruisers of human ideologies and egos for ever, until they sink and drown all the so called 'unwanted ones' in the house of God; whereas the Holy Spirit wants to come into His house to bring life and restoration to broken lives without distinction.

There is something in the human life that is very sensitive to any kind of a change. It is the self-life in every one of us. It is always a battle to yield one's self completely to the Lord in regard to being obedient to whatever He wants us to be doing. Self always wants to take the preeminence, but the closer one gets to the Lord, the humbler he or she becomes, and finds it easier to submit to His will. Without total submission to the Lord, self can destroy the plan of God for our lives.

Sisters, when you meet the Lord face to face; there is no room for self-gratification. There is no room for pride. A life that is stripped of self is sold out to God and to the cause of the Kingdom. The Holy Spirit cautions us here. He says,

"He who thinks he stands should take heed lest he falls" (1 Corinthians 10:12).

The greater the anointing, the easier it is to be prey to pride and self-righteous. We need to watch out. It is easy to become high-minded and proud when you have had an encounter with the Lord. People who are lowly do not fall! Let me say that again, people who feel they are nothing; do not become proud, so they do not fall prey to pride. It is only those who have an encounter with the Lord, who become sometimes conceited, and thereby become victim to pride, except that pride goes before a fall (Proverbs 16:18). Therefore we need to die to self every day.

RUTH OUR EXAMPLE

The example of Ruth is to be emulated by every Christian woman who has a desire to be used of God. Although a widow just like Naomi, she forgot about her pain and clung to this wounded woman of God. She knew Naomi had something she could learn from. She also knew that Naomi's pain was not comparable to hers. Naomi needed someone who spoke her language—the languages of those who know pain, and have learned to comfort others, because they have experienced the same.

"Blessed be God, even the Father of our Lord Jesus Christ, the Father of mercies, and the God of all comforts; *Who comforts us in all our tribulation, that we may be able to comfort them which are in any trouble, by the comfort we ourselves are comforted of God*" (II Corinthians 1:3-4 – emphasis mine).

Ruth was selfless because her heart's desire was to please the Lord and others. She was a humble woman of God who earned her reputation by the life she chose to live and by the decisions she made. She found favor because she followed the advice of her mother-in-law. Hear what Boaz, the kinsman, who later on married her, said,

> "And Boaz answered and said unto her, "it hath been fully showed me, all that thou hast done unto they mother-in-law since the death of thine husband; and how thou hast left thy father and thy mother, and the land of thy nativity, and art come unto a people which thou knewest not heretofore. *The Lord recompense thy work, and a full reward be given thee of the Lord God of Israel, under whose wings thou art come to trust"* (Ruth 2:11-12 – emphasis mine).

This was the testimony given concerning a young woman who was sold out to God.

* * * * * * *

When the apostle Paul, then Saul, met Christ on the road to Damascus, He was wholly transformed and there was no record of his recant from the Christian faith. Rather he grew from faith to glory and was used more mightily than even the disciples. Through Paul we have almost all the epistles written through the inspiration of the Holy Spirit. Some were written while in chains, some in prison, yet it was this same Paul who wrote,

> "But what things were gain to me, those I counted loss for Christ. Yea doubtless, and I count all things but loss for the excellency of the knowledge of Christ Jesus my Lord; for whom I have suffered the loss of all things, and do count them but dung, that I may win Christ, and be found in Him, not having mine own righteousness, ..." (Philippians 3:7-9).

In the book of Galatians, the same apostle gives a clear affirmation of one who has been through the fire, one who lives in the Word, and has a personal intimacy with the King and who is stripped of self.

"I am crucified with Christ; nevertheless I live; yet not I, but Christ lives in me: and the life which I now live in the flesh I live by the faith of the Son of God, who loved me, and gave himself for me" (Galatians 2:20).

The Lord in His Sovereignty has deposited a great wealth of resources in the life of every believer to be used for His service. He has given great talents and different gifts for His use. The reason why some of us have become unprofitable is that we have become spiritually handicapped through ignorance, pride, selfishness, arrogance, personal ambitions, carelessness, indifference, and so many other spiritual ailments. As a result, the Holy Spirit is taking many of us through His boot camps to teach us humility; which will bring us under His authority. He is teaching us how to discipline ourselves as He is fashioning us according to His Word to become useful in His hands.

I believe you know what boot camps do to anybody who takes part in them. The purposes of boot camps are:

- To get young people shape
- To teach them discipline
- To humble them to come under authority
- To toughen them up in order for them to be able to face dangers courageously
- To teach them to live under any circumstances or situation without complaining

The Spirit is speaking expressively to all who desire to be effective in this end-time revival. You and I cannot achieve anything if we have not conquered self. Nevertheless we cannot overcome self in our own self. We need His indwelling presence, and His enabling power to overcome self. Otherwise, He may send you somewhere you would not like to go if self is still ruling. He may ask you to do something unthinkable, and if self is not under control you will not want to do it. You will want your own way and you may suffer the consequences.

A RETROSPECT

Let's review the life of Moses again. He was a man who went through the fire, and who chose to suffer affliction with the people of God rather than to enjoy the pleasures of sin for a season in Egypt as Pharaoh's grandson. He was the Lord's spokesman. He brought the Ten Commandments to the people and read the curses of disobedience and the blessings for obedience. The Lord gave the commandments to him for the people. Moses saw the Lord and was transformed, but there was a part of him that was not submitted to the Master's control—his anger or temper. Self had a foothold to weaken his obedience to God. His anger, at the onset, led him to kill the first Egyptian who was fighting with the Jewish slave, and to the desert. His anger again caused him to break the first commandment written by the hand of the Lord, when he was disappointed that the people had turned into idolatry (Exodus 32:19-20).

"When Moses approached the camp and saw the calf and the dancing, his anger burned and he threw the tablets out of his hands, breaking them to pieces at the foot of the mountain. And he took the calf they had made and burned it in the fire; then he ground it to powder, scattered it on the water and made the Israelites drink it."

Could you have believed this? Moses made the children of Israel to drink the powdered metals? Self plus anger can go even beyond our limited understanding.

The first time the people murmured for water, the Lord asked Moses to use his rod to smite the Rock only once. The Lord gave His people water freely out of the Rock when Moses smote the Rock. This Rock represented Christ who would be smitten only once for the salvation of mankind. However, the second episode of murmuring, complaining, and of the resurgence of hardhearted men and women, produced a different story.

"And the Lord spoke unto Moses, saying, "Take the rod, and gather the assembly together, thou, and Aaron thy brother, and speak ye unto the rock before their eyes; and it shall give forth his water... And Moses took the rod from before the Lord, as he commanded him" (Numbers 20:7-9).

Some folks among the Israelites only knew how to act negatively any time something did not go well, and to destabilize the whole population. Moses, being overwhelmed with their complaint and negativity, could not obey the command to speak to the Rock. This time the 'sleeping giant' of self rose up, and instead of honoring the name and the command of the Lord, Moses did the contrary. He smote the Rock twice instead of speaking to it.

And Moses and Aaron gathered the congregation together before the rock, and he said, 'Hear now, ye rebels; must we fetch you water out of this rock?' And Moses lifted up his hand, and with the rod he smote the rock twice; and the water came out abundantly.... And the Lord spoke unto Moses and Aaron saying, 'because ye believed me not, to sanctify me in the eyes of the children of Israel, therefore ye shall not bring this congregation into the land which I have given them" (Numbers 20:7-12).

The command he received was to go to the rock with the people and speak, nothing more, nothing less. However, self at work in Moses first addressed the people as rebels and showed off a little bit in smiting the rock twice. The Lord's verdict followed. *"You will see the land, but not enter therein."* Moses was later asked to stand on the top of the mountain to view the land of Canaan, but was not able to step there. He died on Mount Pisgah, and the Lord Himself buried him (Deuteronomy 34:1-6).

As said earlier, familiarity always breeds contempt. Moses, I suppose became so accustomed to the presence of God and His dealings with His people, he might have presumed that a little disobedience would do him no harm. But he was mistaken. God is not partial in His dealings with His people. In fact, those of us who have received much shall give a greater account on how we used what He allowed us to have. The closer the presence, the harsher the judgment will be!

As the anointing increases, so will judgment intensify when one deliberately or consistently does what is wrong. I hope we have not forgotten the story of Ananias and Sapphira. It was in the midst of a great manifestation of the Holy Spirit that they died for telling lies (Acts 5:1-11).

The Bible speaks consistently of self, when not dead or stripped destroys lives. Self will always let someone do things contrary to the will of God – hence prevent you and me from entering into the fullness of our inheritance. Self, if not crucified, springs up or revives during pressure. Self is like a pressure cooker. It only takes a little stress, a little pressure, and another dose of frustration to recognize its destructive power. Like Moses, we can be just a stone's throw away from the fulfillment of our vision, and be disqualified.

Self is described in the Bible as the deeds of the flesh. The Apostle Paul says,

> "For they that are after the flesh, do mind the things of the flesh; but they that are after the Spirit, the things of the Spirit. For to be carnally minded is death, but to be spiritually minded, is life and peace. Because the carnal mind is enmity against God; for it is not subject to the law of God, neither indeed can be. So then they that are in the flesh cannot please God" (Romans 8:5-8).

You may ask, *"What kind of message is this? We live under grace."* Beloved, grace does not cancel the holiness of God. This is the reason the Apostle admonishes us through the Holy Spirit to be wholly dedicated and consecrated to the Holy Spirit by allowing ourselves to be living sacrifices of God, living holy lives for His glory.

> "Therefore, I urge you, brothers in view of God's mercy, to offer your bodies as living sacrifices, holy and pleasing to God—this is your spiritual act of worship. Do not conform any longer to the pattern of this world, but be transformed by the renewing of your mind. Then you will be able to test and approve what God's will is—His good, pleasing and perfect will" (Romans 12:1-2).

Paul also states his concerns as he labored with the Master.

"Therefore I do not run like a man running aimlessly; I do not fight like a man beating the air. No, I beat my body and make it my slave so that after I have preached to others, I myself will not be disqualified for the prize" (1 Corinthians 9:26-27 – New International Version).

"I therefore so run, not as uncertainly; so fight I, not as one that beats the air. But I keep under my body, and bring it to subjection: lest that by any means, when I have preached to others, I myself should be a castaway" (I Corinthians 9:26-27 – King James Version).

This scripture always sends chills into my spine. It is a caution to me to be on the right track, allowing the Holy Spirit to help me daily to eradicate the deeds of the flesh so I might end my race with cheers from the clouds of witnesses that are around the throne of God (Hebrews 12:1-2).

These clouds of witnesses are the saints in heaven, who went through the fires, yet did not deny the Lord. They were faithful men and women who lived according to the Word and handled the Word of truth with all reverence and truthfulness. They had real intimacy with the Lord and held His name high in fear and trembling. They were selfless, for their faith was known by all – both in the Old and the New Testaments and our world today.

The King's admonition to all His end-time daughters is plain and clear. *'Be filled with the Spirit, walk in the Spirit, and self will not have a place to gratify itself.'*

"This I say then, Walk in the Spirit, and ye shall not fulfill the lusts of the flesh. For the flesh lusteth against the Spirit, and the Spirit against the flesh: and these are contrary the one to the other; so that ye cannot do the things that ye would. But if ye be led of the Spirit, ye are not under the law. Now the works of the flesh are manifest, which are these, adultery, fornication, uncleanness, lasciviousness, Idolatry, witchcraft, hatred, variance, emulations, wrath, strife, seditions, heresies, envying, murders, drunkenness, revellings and such like: of the which I tell you before, as I have also told you in time past, that they which do such things shall not inherit the kingdom of God. But the fruit of the Spirit is love, joy, peace, longsuffering, gentleness, goodness, faith, meekness, temperance: against such there is no law. *And they that are Christ's have crucified the flesh with the affections and lusts. If we live in the Spirit, let us also walk in the Spirit.* Let us not be desirous of vain glory, provoking one another, envying one another" (Galatians 5:16-26 – emphasis mine).

Ripping off self will help us not to see ourselves better than others. It will also help every woman to maintain the biblical recommendation of being submissive to her husband even if she is used by God more than her husband is. Sisters, we cannot usurp the authority of the man in the home, because of the anointing upon our lives.

QUOTABLE QUOTES

"True spirituality manifests itself in: The desire to be holy rather than happy. The desire to see the honor of God advanced through his life - The desire to carry his cross - The desire to see everything from God's viewpoint - The desire to die right rather than live wrong - The desire to see others advance at his own expense - The desire to make eternity-judgments instead of time judgments."

A.W. Tozer

[12]

WOMEN WHO LIVE UNDER AUTHORITY

(Humility and Submission)

❖

"...All of you, clothe yourselves with humility toward one another, because, "God opposes the proud but gives grace to the humble." Humble yourselves, therefore, under God's mighty hand, that He may lift you up in due time. ... Be self-controlled and alert. Your enemy the devil prowls around like a roaring lion looking for someone to devour" (I Peter 5:5-6, 8).

"Obey your leaders and submit to their authority. They keep watch over you as men who must give an account. Obey them so that their work will be a joy, not a burden, for that would be of no advantage to you" (Hebrews 13:17).

In a world full of competitions, every Christian must guard against self-sufficiency, conservative spirit, and 'do it all yourself' mentality. No one person can stand alone. We all need to be accountable to someone. We all need someone, from whom we can draw inspiration, strength, and encouragement when the going gets tough. We all need someone on whose shoulder we can cry when pain, rejection, and hardship settle in. We all need someone with whom we can celebrate success, and rejoice over miracles accomplished without being puffed up in the spirit. We all need someone. And every believer needs to be under some kind of authority for accountability, and for protection.

In a world where everyone wants to be the boss, it is very hard to submit to another's control. However, I say, that to have authority means one has the legal right or power to enforce obedience positively. When we have not learned to submit to any authority in our lives, we cannot have legal rights to enforce obedience, either in the spirit realm or in the physical.

Jesus gave His disciples power over demons and the forces of the enemy before Pentecost. Why were they not effective in their ministry before Pentecost? There was a problem. They were bickering, and fighting over who would be the boss all the time. However, the story changed after Jesus ascended. They all met together under the leadership of Christ's command, and His 'invisible' presence to wait for the indwelling of the Holy Spirit. And the glory came. Signs and wonders became a part of their ministry, because it was part and parcel of the great commission. A diligent study of the book of Acts, gives us the answer to their success—they were all under the authority of Christ, of the Holy Spirit, and of the Leaders placed over them.

Submission to a known, direct or indirect authority over an individual is a God-given command given to every human being on earth. Submission leads to total obedience, and obedience leads to success and fulfillment. There would be no confusion in homes, schools, offices, nations, and anywhere, when people learn to submit and live according to the God given assignment given them. Harmony, peace and happiness would be the outcome.

There is a Biblical event which leads to our point. Remember the centurion who came to Jesus? He knew the power of delegated authority. One of his servants was sick. He came to Jesus to ask Him to heal him. Jesus, point blankly assured him He was more than willing to go with him to heal the servant. Conversely, he said to the Lord Jesus,

> "Lord, I do not deserve to have you come under my roof. But say the word, and my servant will be healed. **For I myself am a man under authority,** with soldiers under me. I tell this one, 'Go.' And he goes; and that one 'Come' and he comes. I say to my servant, 'Do this,' and he does it" (Matthew 8:8-9 – emphasis mine).

It is required of every child of God, and especially all the end-time daughters of the King, to learn to willingly submit completely to God, to spiritual leaders, to husbands, and to any kind of authority God has placed over us.

UNDER GOD'S AUTHORITY

> "Not everyone who says to Me, 'Lord, Lord,' will enter the kingdom of heaven, but only he who does the will of My Father who is in heaven. Many will say to Me on that day, 'Lord, Lord, did we not prophesy in Your name, and in Your name drive out demons and perform many miracles?' Then I will tell them plainly, 'I never knew you. Away from me, you evil-doers!'" (Matthew 7:21-23).

Being under God's authority means we must yield completely to His will, and His control. Starting from the book of Genesis, we see clearly the blessings, the power, and authority Adam and Eve had being under God's government and authority. However, when they willingly disobeyed God's command and ate the forbidden fruit, the whole world fell under a curse. As long as they were obedient and lived according to God's command, they enjoyed freedom, comfort, peace, protection and abundance from His presence. But the moment they chose voluntarily to turn against God's simple command, "Do not touch," they forfeited all the blessings God had purposed for them. God drove them out of the garden of divine provision and blessings to face a sin cursed world of pain and toil of their own making.

Their first son Cain, chose to rebel against God's desired will—a blood sacrifice, pointing to the work of redemption Christ would accomplish, and restore what we lost in Adam in God's due time. On the other hand, Abel chose to live under God's authority, and to obey His command. And even though he died doing God's will, the Bible testified of him as being righteous—which means: being in right standing with God.

Jesus, the Son of God, came to John the Baptist to be baptized. Why? He could have gone ahead with His ministry without going through the religious formalities in His day. Nevertheless, God in the flesh, submitted Himself to the established order of repentance through baptism. Soon after His baptism, the heavens opened, and God's Son was officially introduced to the world, and confirmed to John and his disciples. He had full authority as the Son of man to minister to men, because He submitted to His Father's institution, and to His fore-runner, John the Baptist. He had full authority over the devil, because He did not succumb to the devil's temptation to display His Son-ship (Matthew 4).

Disobedience removes a child of God from God's protective care.

Jesus also said to the Pharisees of His day, *"What I see My Father do, that l do"* (John 5:19-21; 6:25, 38-40). His prayer in the garden of Gethsemane is a picture of the will of the Father completely absorbed in that of the Son. *"Father, if it is possible, let this cup pass over me. Nevertheless, not My will, but Yours be done,"* Jesus prayed (Luke 22:39-44). Jesus is our perfect example. He always did what the Father did. We are admonished to emulate Christ.

"Do nothing out of selfish ambition or vain conceit, but in humility consider others better than yourselves. Each of you should look not only to your own interests, but also to the interests of others. Your attitude should be the same as that of Christ Jesus: Who, being in the very nature God, did not consider equality with God something to be grasped, but made Himself nothing, taking the very nature of a servant, being made in human likeness. And being found in appearance as a man, He humbled Himself and became obedient to death—even death on a cross! Therefore God exalted Him to the highest place and gave Him the name that is above every name, that at the name of Jesus every knee should bow, in heaven and on earth and under the earth, and every tongue confess that Jesus Christ is Lord, to the glory of God the Father" (Philippians 2:3-11).

Yielding under God's control implies that we do not set up our own agendas, and plans, then ask Him to agree with us and bless them. This does not imply that we must not plan, or have a goal in life. It actually means that every agenda, every goal or vision, any planned effort for the kingdom must be submitted to Him first for His guidance and His approval.

"Why do you call Me, 'Lord, Lord,' and do not do what I say? I will show you what he is like who come to Me and hears My words and puts them into practice. He is like a man who building a house, who dug down deep and laid the foundation on rock. When a flood came, the torrent struck that house but could not shake it, because it was well built. But the one who hears My words and does not put them into practice is like a man who built a house on the ground without foundation. The moment the torrent struck that house, it collapsed and its destruction was complete" (Luke 6:46-49).

MY OWN EXAMPLE

I was working at the Teen Challenge center in Mississippi. Things weren't going on as I expected, yet I wanted to stay put because of the financial strain I was going through in supporting my two younger sons. Three times, the Lord spoke to me to leave, but I wasn't going to listen. You see, it is easy to heed the voice of God when you know where your next meal is coming from. But when you are uncertain about your future, and that of your family, you question whatever voice you hear, and whatever dream you may have.

On the other hand, I felt restless most of the time, without peace of mind. Then the Lord broke through and gave me a revelation that changed my attitude on how I should take His command serious. I woke up abruptly in the middle of the night. I knew something was wrong. I began to pray asking the Lord what the problem was, and continued to pray in the spirit for a while. All of a sudden I fell in to a deep sleep for about 30 minutes. And this is what I saw:

"I found myself on top of different ranges of mountains which connected to each other. These were extraordinary mountains, because they were covered with white glazed substance like snow, but really inexplicably beautiful and glorious. They stretched as far as toward the heavens where the glory dwelt. The roads on the mountains were paved and all the people coming from all corners, traveling on the roads, were driving the most beautiful cars I've never seen on earth. They were all dressed in white traveling toward one direction – upward.

I saw that I was in a car with my husband heading towards the highest peak touching the heavenly realm. We were supposed to cross a bridge before transitioning to the other side of the glory beyond. When we got to the middle part of the bridge, my husband stopped. He looked terrified, and didn't want to go further. I asked him why he stopped. He told me someone was blocking his view from going forward. I looked, and there in front of us was a human monster hanging on one side of the bridge. I recognized the face.

"Go forward, darling. We have come this far and we cannot retreat." I was encouraging him to go forward in Jesus name, but he wouldn't.

"This person (name withheld) doesn't want me to go forward. He is terrorizing me. ….." Geoffrey kept on telling me.

All of a sudden, he turned in reverse; and down we went into the valley and hit the ground. It was a hard fall. When I came to myself, still in the dream, my husband was gone. All around me was total darkness. The only light I saw was on top of the mountain, and its surrounding towns. I began crying and calling out to find my husband. But he was gone. Someone told me, "He's gone to glory."

I made my way toward the town. I saw many Teen Challenge buses parked by the side of the road waiting for people to board. Each one of them had an inscription on it indicating where the center was. I decided to enter into the Mississippi Teen Challenge bus which was in front of me. At that moment, I heard a voice calling from the direction of the mountain. It resounded so loud "Monica, do not enter into the bus again. God is going to take you higher. Return to the mountain. Return to the mountain top. He is taking you higher. ...."

I did not want to listen to what I was hearing. Going from one van to the other, I heard the same voice telling me not to enter, but to go back to the mountain. Very confused, I turned around and headed toward the mountain. On my way to the mountain, I saw a young lady who was dying in a house in Togo. I was told she was going to die because of her sin. I pleaded for her life, and was assured that because I interceded for her, she won't die but the baby she was carrying would die as a sign to me of what I had witnessed.

At that moment, I heard the same voice calling out to me to run back to the mountain. When I got to the bottom of the mountain, I perceived that the mountain was huge and higher than what I had expected. Then I heard the voice of my husband beyond where the glory was, saying, "Darling, go up! Go higher. The Lord is taking you higher. Do not look back, go forward, and go forward. ..."

As I began climbing, I found out it wasn't going to be an easy climb. It was steep, rocky, and dangerous, but the voice of the Lord was cheering me to go forward. Chained on me, was a long train of men, women, and young people that I was supposed to take up to the mountain. Initially, at the onset on the climb, I saw a wooden sword in the shape of a cross, in my hand, but as I climbed gradually in pain, yet determined, the wooden sword turned into a real sword. My gaze was fixed on the glory, although it was painful to climb. Just some few yards to the top of the mountain, where we retreated, I woke up with the sound of the same voice I had heard earlier saying, "Monica, don't go back, go higher. The Lord is taking you higher .... "

With this revelation, I left Teen Challenge of Mississippi. Life hasn't been all that easy for me. Really, the climb has been steep and rocky, but I am steady! I questioned and questioned again whether the dream was of God or from the devil. I knew also that it was from the Lord, because the girl in the dream was spared from death, but the baby she got out of wed-lock died just as I was told in the revelation. I have decided to walk hand in hand with Him. And I believe all will be well. After everything is said and done, one of these days, I will see the faces of those I had carried to the mountains in my travail. It's going to be all right with Jesus.

Since then, I have had many Teen Challenge doors opened for me. Anytime I wanted to make the decision to work there, my heart will begin to pound, and this revelation will re-surface, and I will literally hear the Lord speak to me. "No!" It has been scary, yet. In the midst of my confusion and struggle, the Lord spoke to me,

"Monica, when I tell you to make certain decisions, I am not trying to make your life hard or miserable. No! I am setting you up for a blessing. On the other hand, anything I ask you to do is better than your best. Your best is temporal. My best is eternal. My promise is to make you prosperous and not a curse.

The only thing I request is total obedience. Often times I will require things of you that I won't require of others. I won't explain, and you can't understand it. When you obey, you may or may not see the result immediately. But remember: I am God, and I have a unique plan for your life that I will never stereotype or photocopy. All will be well. Just trust Me! ..."

The last struggle I had was my battle with immigration. Although I am on Pastoral Care at the County hospital as a volunteer, I had to work with my denomination before obtaining a permanent status. I had tried many times to find a church within our denomination to work with me in California to continue the process with immigration, but it wasn't going to be possible. And so, my last resort was to go back to work with Teen Challenge. The door flew wide open. I stepped into it without thinking. Although I felt uneasy, I talked to myself: *"Hey Monica, you've got to forget about this revelation, and learn to survive in America. No one will take care of your needs in America. After all, no one knows you here, bla, bla, bla."* Still I had no peace. I went ahead and moved into one of the centers in San Jose. I still had no peace of mind. I could feel the Lord tugging on my heart. I only argued with Him for a long time about my situation.

I love Teen Challenge. This institution is the most successful one among all the rehabs ever founded, because it gives people the solution—which is Christ, and not seven or ten steps to get out of drugs. Yet my human mind wanted to do what I wanted, and not what the Lord had asked me to do. I worked from July to September in such peace-less condition. I pretended being happy. The people loved me, but there was something that wasn't clicking in my inner most being. Any one I told this revelation to, told me I should forget about it, and that God will not punish me or strike me dead for working in Teen Challenge. I knew that, but that didn't sound right in my spirit. I struggled for quite a while. Then one day The Lord spoke to me.

It was 2:23 in the morning. I had fasted for two days and prayed this particular night till twelve. I then went to sleep. I was dreaming of a heavy torrential outpouring of rain. It came down with lightening and thunder. The loudness of the clashing thunder and lightening jolted me out of the bed. I thought it was real. At that moment, I heard the most thunderous voice I had ever heard in my life. It shook my bed. Lighting flashed through the room. I was terrified and went under the covers. Then He said,

> "Who brought you here, Monica? Was it yourself? Tell Me or was it I? When I brought you here, did you bring any money which was yours? Did I not provide everything which was necessary for you to come here? And when I led you out of Teen Challenge of Mississippi, did I not take care of you? Why do you act as if your life is in your own hands? Why do you depend on what others say, and obey their command, without asking My opinion first? Can you trust Me? Would you trust Me to take you through this journey? Then trust Me! I am your God. …………….."

I broke down crying. When I came to myself, I sat up and thought, "Has it been raining?" No. Everywhere was calm, and it had not even rained. I knew the Lord was speaking to me to leave. That was it. I left Teen Challenge Alum Rock with the excuse that I was sick, because I was afraid of being ridiculed. Although I was sick during the time of my resignation, I used that as my excuse to get out without giving the glory to the Lord. As a result of that, another proposal for Teen challenge came up. I almost succumbed to this one too, because of immigration and my financial problems. This time, the Lord gave me boldness to establish the truth, and to tell the District officials what actually is happening. When I did, He rained peace; I say supernatural peace upon my heart, because I have not known such peace since my husband died, and we came here. Then the Lord said to me,

> "Monica, My thoughts are not your thoughts, neither are My ways your ways. You think like human, and you act like human, but I am not human. I AM GOD. I brought you here, and I will fulfill all that I said concerning you so that I alone may receive the glory and not you. You tend to listen to human advice anytime you are confronted with a decision. You forget that your ways are not yours. They are Mine to guide. Your paths have never been yours to take. I have guided you right from childhood to this day. Why don't you sit calm and see what I am going to do with you. You are mine, and mine you will be forever. I will guide you. I will accomplish all my plans and desires for your life. You will see it and rejoice in Me. I have never left you, and I will never leave you. You think I did when everything fell apart. No! I am still your God. Stand still and see my salvation. Have I ever failed you? Never! You may think so, but I AM always faithful… You and the children I gave you are for signs and wonders to nations, to churches, and as many as I would bring closer to you………"

Although, I have been misunderstood by many, I know who my Lord is. Right from the time I gave my heart to Him at the age of ten, His hand has been very strong on me, especially, when it has to do with His direction. Now, I am satisfied and happy with what I am doing at the hospital, and with writing. I am also content with the ministry to the older singles and widows, the prayer ministry, and whatever He has called me to do. I don't have to struggle to be someone else. It is spiritually dangerous.

****

Dear sisters, being under His authority is the best things that can ever happen to any child of God. You see, Balaam thought he could use his preconceived stubborn ideas to manipulate God to agree with his selfish ambition to gain filthy lucre. He forgot that money can blindfold even the just, and stubbornness is as the sin of witchcraft; moreover, witches are not suffered to live. He desired to die a righteous death; rather he was killed with the sword.

Someone said, "Praying about the known will of God is rebellion against God." Yielding to the known will of God without complaint becomes a mighty weapon in the hand of a believer to defeat self, the devil, and the world's influence of complacency.

UNDER HUMAN AUTHORITY

"Everyone must submit himself to the governing authorities, for there is not authority except that which God has established by God. Subsequently, he who rebels against authority is rebelling against what God has instituted, and those who do so will bring judgment on themselves" (Romans 13:1-2).

The story of Mary and Joseph sheds light on being under God's authority and human authority as well. Here is a young virgin, who had found favor with God. She received a direct visit from God through an angel with a message that God Almighty, the Creator of Heaven and earth, was going to make His bed in her womb. She was going to become pregnant, and bring forth God's Son. Mary accepted this assignment knowing the consequences. Maybe Joseph would repudiate her. That was obvious. Maybe she could be stoned. Exactly! This is according to the law. Maybe she would be driven out from society. None of these actually bothered her. She only desired to be the instrument of Israel's redemption. Her response to the angel was frantic and plain, full of faith and hope for her future. "Let it be to me according to your word." (Please read Luke 1:26-38) She would take God at His word; knowing God was able to keep her from harm.

Then Joseph comes to the scene. He sees Mary pregnant. He did not care much about who did what to Mary. He cared about his reputation, because he was a righteous man. He wanted to divorce Mary secretly to avoid public disgrace. That was his intentions. But God wouldn't stop there. He speaks to Joseph in a dream, confirming His word to Mary. Not only did God clarify the situation around Mary's pregnancy, He would place Mary and the God Son under Joseph's authority as well. He was told,

"Joseph son of David, do not be afraid to take Mary home to be your wife, because what is conceived in her womb is from the Holy Spirit. She will give birth to a Son, *and you are to give him the name Jesus*, because He will save His people from their sins" (Matthew 1:20-21 – emphasis mine).

"What is the deal here?" you may ask. Joseph's authority over Mary, even though the marriage was not consummated until after the Baby Jesus was born, was God's way of placing Mary and His Son under divine authority for protection, and preservation. His Son would learn obedience under human parents; and especially from an earthly carpenter father. Jesus would literally see His mission on earth through the wood and the nail "daddy Joseph" used in his work.

Each day, as He worked with him, from a young child till He reached the age thirty; Jesus saw His destiny through Joseph's trade. He became a carpenter, who not only made new furniture, but who also repaired broken stuff. Indeed, He came to make all things new, and to repair broken lives. Yet He learned obedience from Mary. His earthly mother subjected to Joseph for accountability, for protection, and for legitimacy.

"Do nothing out of selfish ambition or vain conceit, but in humility consider others better than yourselves. Each of you should not look only to your own interest, but also to the interests of others. Your attitude should be the same as that of Christ Jesus: Who, being in the very nature God, did not consider equality with God as something to be grasped, but made Himself nothing, taking the very nature of a servant, being found in human likeness. And being found in appearance as a man, He humbled Himself and became obedient to death—even the death of the cross! Therefore God exalted Him to the highest place and gave Him the name that is above every name, that at the name of Jesus every knee should bow, in heaven and on earth and under the earth, and every tongue confess that Jesus Christ is Lord, to the glory of God the Father" (Philippians 2:3-11).

In the case of Paul the Apostle, the Lord had asked him to go to Jerusalem. He knew it wasn't going to be easy for him. Prophet Agabus' prophecy confirmed what he already knew, yet the brethren tried to oppose him from going to Jerusalem—not willing for him to suffer as prophesied. Although Paul's obedience cost him almost his life in the hands of the Jews in Jerusalem, his mission—to be a witness to kings, as predetermined by the Holy Spirit (Acts 9:1-

16; Acts 20 & 2) was consummated as he stood to testify before kings, governors; and the Jewish leaders; fulfilling the word of the Lord spoken concerning him. Hence, Paul could boldly say, "I was not disobedient unto the heavenly vision" (Acts 26:19).

Remember sister: Being in God's will does not exempt any believer from suffering. In living our lives to please the Lord, we can also confidently affirm with Paul,

> "And herein do I exercise myself, to have a conscience void of offense toward God, and toward men" (Acts 24:16)

The Lord said to me one day, "Monica, the best way in knowing My will is doing My will as written in My Love Letter (The Word) to you. Then pursue what I have called you to do for My Glory. Being in My will does not exempt you from pain, persecutions, trials and rejections. It is an illusion for My children to think that being in My will means every thing will be smooth and creamy. Rather, My will may lead to untold sufferings and even death for My glory. No matter what happens, see to it that you do not harbor hate or bitterness; anger and unforgiveness. Instead, turn your bitterness and hurt in to love and compassion. This will bring about the beauty of My Son, in whose likeness you were predestined to be. There's a cross to carry. There are burdens to bear. There are rivers to cross and fires to quench. There are many thorns along the way. The climb may be steep and tiresome, but be still and calm. I did not promise you beautiful roses without thorns, neither pure honey on the milky-way beyond the galaxies without bee stings. But I promised you My Presence; and that will never fail (Isaiah 43:2). Don't look for an easy way out of life. Look rather for My heart. The joy of knowing My heart and being in the center of My will, will alleviate the pain that comes in the package of doing My will."

"Whosoever will come after me, let him deny himself, take up his cross and follow Me" (Mark 8:33).

I believe a lot of books have been written about this subject, and I pray that the Lord will quicken us to find help where it is necessary in order to live in humility under His protection and His blessings. The only time God would override human authority is when it goes against His known and revealed will to His children. Please, read the story of Shadrach, Meshach and Abednego (Daniel 3:1-30); and Daniel in the lion's den (Daniel 6).

Last of all, I would say this: There are four classes of women in the house of God.

The Athaliahs – They are those who want to usurp authority by all means. They push their way through things, and want to control even God's appointed authority. They take revenge. They are controllers, usurpers, and they care less who they hurt. They hurt others themselves, yet they hold offenses, and will never forgive anyone who steps on their toes. They take what is not theirs, because they want to rule by all means (2 Kings 11).

The Jezebels – These are very religious. They are instigators of evil. They are very cunning and deceitful. They are very charismatic, fearless and strong. They never come under any authority whatsoever. They have power to do evil to every one except the devil. They are there to ruin men's lives. They come in subtlety with the intention of ruining the lives of God's people. Control is their weapon (1 Kings 18, 19; 21:1-19; 2 Kings 9:30-37). They control their husbands. They control their leaders. They control others, and sometimes they think they control everyone's destiny; and even theirs.

The Miriams – They are God's children. They are the ones who know the mind of God, and even that of the pastors. They are the core leaders. They are the altar ministers in local assemblies. They are the zealous, the eloquent, and the learned ones. They have almost all the gifts of the Spirit. They are wonderful women of God, yet lack respect for God's authority. They are always negative when it comes to submission and receiving counsel. They think that once they hear from God, they have the power to speak against God's appointed authorities. Sisters, a little bit of pride, a little bit of self, and a little more of power can wreck the life of a mighty woman of God (Numbers 12). Most Christians are guilty of this.

The Marys and the Ruths – These are behind the scene instruments. They boast of nothing. They are submissive, and obedient. They pray underground. They labor under cover. They have seen a lot in life. No one notices them, yet without these, the world's history would not have been written. They have sacrificed a lot, and gained a little for themselves. They walk about with the scars of their Beloved, who is their King. They know what to do, and how to do it at the right time without causing conflict. They accept God's will without complaints. They will not strive. They will work hard, until they see the salvation of others completed in Christ. The will of their Beloved is their priority, and the welfare of others is their hearts cry.

Beloved, rebellion can take someone farther than they want to go. Which one of these women are we going to be? May the Lord grant us hearts of submission to His authority, and the grace to humbly serve those He's placed over us. Then and only then, can we have legal rights to enforce obedience in others.

The seven sons of Sceva in the book of Acts 19:11-17, who had nothing to do with Christ, and were not under the authority, or the government of God, is one example we need to consider. Interestingly, the demons in the possessed man could discern to know that they were neither under Christ' authority nor that of any human being. They had no rights to tell them to leave the man, and were severely beaten by demons. Wow! That's really scary. "A word to the wise is enough" says the sage.

QUOTABLE QUOTES

"Pride is the ground in which all the other sins grow, and the parent from which all the other sins come."

William Barclay (1907-1978)

[13]

WOMEN WHO ARMED THEMSELVES FOR BATTLE

(Zealousness For The Kingdom)

❖

"On your feet, daughter of Zion! Be threshed of chaff, be refined of dross. I'm remaking you into a people invincible, into God's juggernaut to crush the godless peoples. You'll bring their plunder as holy offerings to God, their wealth to the Master of the earth" (Micah 4:13, The Message).

"As you go, preach this message: 'The kingdom of heaven is near.' Heal the sick, raise the dead, cleanse those who have leprosy, and drive out demons. Freely you have received, freely give" (Matthew 10:7-8).

It is time for the King's daughters to go to battle. It is time for the daughters of Zion to go to war against the enemy that wants to destroy our marriages, robs us of our husbands, and to take our children captive. It is time for us to rise up like Esther to say no to the forces of evil that is sowing discords in our churches. It is high time we rise up and fight against drugs, alcohol, crimes in our neighborhoods, and our nations on our knees. It is time for us to preach Christ and Him crucified, buried and resurrected, seated at the right hand of God the Father. It is high time to heal the sick, raise the dead, mend broken hearts, and proclaim the soon coming of our Lord and Savior Jesus Christ. We have the power. We have the weapons, and we have a mighty backing. We will win if we will stand up and fight.

These armies we have been talking about have received a command from the Great Commander in Chief to go forth to battle. It sounded somehow like this: "FORWARD EVER! BACKWARD NEVER! YOU KNOW NO DEFEAT! I AM THE COMMANDING OFFICER, RIGHT! MATCH ON, MATCH ON TO VICTORY!" Jesus declared this when He gave us power over all the powers of the enemy.

> "I saw Satan fall like lightning. I have given you authority to trample on snakes and scorpions and to overcome all the power of the enemy; nothing will harm you (Luke 19:18-19).

Jesus Himself went to Hades, took the keys we handed over to the enemy the day Adam and Eve fell, and sounded the news loud to all who believe in Him.

> "All power is given unto me in heaven and in earth. Go ye therefore, and teach all nations, baptizing them in the name of the Father, and of the Son, and of the Holy Ghost; teaching them to observe all things

whatsoever I have commanded you; and lo, I am with you always, even unto the end of the world. Amen" (Matthew 28:18-20).

"Go into all the world and preach the good news to all creation. ... And these signs shall follow them that believe; In my name shall they cast out devils; they shall speak with new tongues; they shall take up serpents, and if they drink any deadly thing, it shall not hurt them; they shall lay hands on the sick and they shall recover" (Mark 16:15, 17-18).

In the book of 2 Samuel 11, we read that it was time for kings to go to war, but David stayed home. Staying back after having been equipped (anointed) by the Lord to go to war to bring victory to his nation, cost David a child, his family, almost his throne, and caused a whole lot of other problems in his own family. King David's problem at that time is the same as ours today. Let's take an inventory with King David. It starts with:

a) **Carelessness** – Whether his people died or not, King David did not care much about it. How much do you care about your family's salvation? What about your neighbor next door who needs someone to minister to him or her, and the single mother or widow who doesn't have anybody to talk to? And what about the assignment the Lord has given us—the family of God under our care? Do we take time to pray and intercede for each member of our congregation, ministries, or our businesses?

b) **Indifference** – King David was sleeping or resting while he needed to go to war. The Bible warns against indifference. This is a real problem in our world today. "It's not my problem" we say. It is our problem. If our world turns upside down because we failed to do our jobs as salt and light, we will never be exempt from the outcome.

c) **Lust** – He desired the wife of another as he strolled on the top of his house. The very place of his lust was where his own son, Absalom, took advantage of and slept with all his father's concubines. Do you know why we have lots of divorces, marital problems today? Most of them are caused by lust - lusting after other flesh through pornography — lusting after strange flesh. Many times, we think lust has to do with only immorality, but what about lusting after worldly things - things that do not satisfy.

d) **Selfishness** - He coveted the wife of Uriah. He was not satisfied with all that the Lord had blessed him with. He lusted after Bathsheba, another man's wife, because he was not content with all the other wives he already had. That is selfishness. Why are there so many problems in nations, homes and everywhere? Guess. Selfishness is what is killing the world—our comforts at the expense of someone else.

e) **Deceit** – King David, brought Uriah home so he could sleep with his wife, in order to shift responsibility for impregnating Bathsheba. Uriah, being a man of valor, and who had the heart of God, would not sleep with his own wife at this time of war. He wasn't going to enjoy himself while his people battled alone.

f) **Wickedness** – Wickedness took hold of David's heart when he planned to eliminate the godly husband of the woman. How do we term wickedness? When a Christian does not obey God to do what he or she has been called to do, God calls it wickedness. Please, read the parable of the talents in Matthew 25:14-30. The servant, who failed to use the talent of opportunities given him by the master to do well, was thrown into outer darkness. The master called him 'a wicked servant.'

g) **Murder** – Uriah was killed. David shed innocent blood to cover up his sin. How much blood do we share everyday as Christians? A lot! How many lives do we take with lies, deception, envy, evil speaking, and false accusations? Unbelievable! The Bible says that anyone who hates his brother without cause is a murderer (I John 3:15). Read also Matthew 5:21-22.

h) **Pretentiousness** – After killing the husband, King David acted as if nothing had happened between him and the woman. Pretending to be something when we are not is very dangerous. The Church of Laodicea was reprimanded by Christ for being pretentious and deceptive (Revelation 3:14-22).

i) **Giving occasion to the enemy** – David gave the enemy an occasion to blaspheme the Name of the Lord of host. How? It brought death to the innocent, and disgrace to the Kingdom. Although King David paid for the consequences of his carelessness, his children carried the rest of the curse for his wrong choices.

DRESS UP AND BE ALERT!

Daughters of the King, we have not been through what we've been through to settle back and enjoy our Christian lives while the enemy is working tirelessly; taking many captive and destroying lives. We have been refined and armed for a purpose, and if we do not launch out into the deep, we can become like King David. When the enemy prevails, we shall not be spared.

After being trained, a soldier needs first to put on his or her uniform, before going to battle. The enemy through subtlety has ridden the King's daughters of our beautiful apparel, with which our Father clothed us. Our Father clothed us with garments of many colors like that of Joseph, when we gave our lives to Him, because He had a purpose for our lives. Christ was stripped naked so we might be clothed. In the Bible, colors have various significances.

- **White describes Majesty** - "As I looked, "thrones were set in place, and the Ancient of Days took His seat. His clothing was as **white** as snow; the hair of His head was **white** like wool. His throne was flaming with fire, and its wheels were all ablaze" (Daniel 7:9).

    Of Glory: "...Jesus took with him Peter, James and John the brother of James, and led them up a high mountain by themselves. There He was transfigured before them. His face shone like the sun, and His clothes became as **white** as the light" (Matthew 17:1-2; read also Mark 9:3; Luke 9:27; Revelation 1:13, 14).

    Of Purity - "Yet you have a few people in Sardis who have not soiled their clothes. They will walk with Me, dressed in **white**, for they are worthy. He who overcomes will, like them, be dressed in **white**. I will never blot out his (her) name from the book of life, but will acknowledge his (her) name before My Father and His holy angels" (Revelation 3:4-5 – emphasis mine).

    Of Victory - "After this I looked and there before me was a great multitude that no one could count, from every nation, tribe, people and language, standing before the throne and in front of the Lamb. They were wearing **white** robes and were holding palm branches in their hands..." (Revelation 7:9).

    Of Forgiveness and Cleansing of sins - "Come now, let us reason together," says the Lord. "Though your sins are like scarlet, they shall be as white as snow; though they be red as crimson, they shall be as wool" (Isaiah 1:18).

    Of Completion: "Then I saw a great white throne and Him who sat on it. Earth and sky fled from His presence, and there was no place for them" (Revelation 20:11).

- **Green is descriptive of Fruitfulness,** "The righteous will flourish like a palm tree, they will grow like a cedar of Lebanon; planted in the house of the Lord, they will flourish in the courts of our God. They will still bear fruit in old age; they will stay **fresh and green**, proclaiming, 'The Lord is upright; He is my Rock, and there is no wickedness in Him." (Psalms 92:12-15; also Psalms 1),

    Of Spiritual Privileges - "The Lord is my Shepherd, I shall not want. He makes me lie down in **green pastures**, He leads me beside quiet waters, He restores my soul" (Psalms 23:1-3; also Jeremiah 11:16).

    Of Spiritual Life - "But I am like a **green** olive tree in the house of God: I trust in the mercy of God for ever and ever" (Psalms 52:8).

- **Purple describes Royalty:** "But Gideon told them, "I will not rule over you, nor will my son rule over you. The Lord will rule over you." And he said, I do have one request, that each of you give me an earring from your share of the plunder." ... They answered, "We'll be glad to give them." So they spread out a garment, and each man threw a ring from his plunder onto it. The weight of the gold rings he asked for came to seventeen hundred shekels, not counting the ornaments, the pendants and the **purple garments worn by the kings** of Midian ... (Judges 8:23-26).

    Of Wealth and **Luxury**: "There was a rich man who was dressed in purple and fine linen and lived in luxury every day" (Luke 16:19; and also Revelation

17:4). We are Royalties, rich in Christ, and blessed by God.

- **Blue describes Divine Revelations and Heavenly Character** (Exodus 24:10; 28:31). Our Father, the King, has endowed us with divine wisdom and knowledge of His divine mysteries, and day after day we are being transformed into becoming like Christ.

These are few of the colorful clothing (privileges and inheritances) we have in Christ. But the enemy, just like the brothers of Joseph, tainted the royal robe of many colors with other blood, so we will not be recognizable and useable. Nevertheless, the news of renewal is already in the air. Listen to the voice of the Spirit, and let us get rid of that tainted robe of red, a type of God's wrath on us; of black, which symbolizes sinfulness, and of ashes, sorrow and rejection, shame, and the rest of its neighbors.

* * * * * * *

Right now, many of us are in labor; so to speak, ready to bring forth the glory of the Lord and the revival in the land. We are not going to heaven to do that. Heaven is already filled with the glory of the Lord. Heaven doesn't need revival. Heaven is not the birthing place. We are going to bring forth everything the enemy stole from us. We're going to take back what the devil stole from us with full force in the power of the Holy Spirit, who resides in us. It is going to be done in the presence of our enemy.

O daughter of the King, allow the Holy Spirit to induce the birthing pain to birth your destiny; your passion and your desire; and to clothe you with divine obsession. Clothe yourself with the heart of your Father. Cry out in pain for the 'child' is ready to be born by the Holy Spirit.

"Be in pain, and labor to bring forth, O daughter of Zion, like a woman in travail; for now shall thou go forth out of the city, and thou shall dwell in the field, and thou shall go even to Babylon, there thou shall be delivered; there the Lord shall redeem thee from the hands of thine enemies" (Micah 4:10).

Do you see the sequence of events the Father is prophesying concerning you? First, it states that the 'delivery' will not take place in the hiding. She shall go forth out of the city, and shall dwell in the field. Look! The fields are already white for harvest! Your divine destiny is already ripened.

Inside chambers describe limitations and boundaries. The Lord says your restoration will be in the open fields for everyone to see the Lord being glorified. You see, revival never stays in-doors. True revival goes world wide. It travels to the camp of its enemies.

Secondly, you will bring forth in 'Babylon'. Why Babylon? You may ask. Do you remember the fall of Lucifer was figuratively compared to that of the fall of Babylon? Read Isaiah 14:12-17 and Ezekiel 28:11-17.

Yes, the very enemy who wanted to destroy the heart of God in us is going to see the birth of our destiny. He will see it and tremble like the day Christ rose from the dead. It was the day his head was crushed and redemption came to the entire human race through the willingness of one woman, Mary, who made herself available to birth the God Son. Everybody will see the anointing upon many women and their call to the ministry culminated. All 'women ministries haters' shall bring glory to the Lord who is doing this. This is the reason He is taking us out, and arming us for battle.

"Arise and thresh, O daughter of Zion; for I will make thine horn iron, and I will make thy hoofs brass: and thou shall beat in pieces many people; and

I will consecrate their gain unto the Lord and I their substances unto the Lord of the earth" (Micah 4:13).

Daughter of the King, get rid of those false and inadequate weapons of self sufficiency, and arm yourself with the whole armor of God. They have already been provided. Our weapons are mighty to destroy every stronghold of the enemy, and to remove all obstacles in the way. Put them on and let us go out to battle.

The Bible enumerates the weapons we need in order for us to be successful in this combat.

"For though we live in the world, we do not wage war as the world does. The weapons we fight with are not the weapons of the world. On the contrary, they have divine power to demolish strongholds. We demolish arguments and every pretension that sets itself up against the knowledge of God, and we take captive every thought to make it obedient to Christ. And we will be ready to punish every act of disobedience, once your obedience is complete" (II Corinthians 10:3-6).

"Finally, be strong in the Lord and in His mighty power. Put on the full armor of God so that you can take your stand against the devil's schemes. For our struggle is not against flesh and blood, but against the rulers, against the spiritual forces of evil in the heavenly realms. Therefore put on the full armor of God so that when the day of evil comes, you may be able to stand your ground, and after you have done everything, to stand. Stand firm then, with the belt of truth buckled around your waist, with the breastplate of righteousness in place, and with your feet fitted with the readiness that comes from the gospel of peace. In addition to all this, take up the shield of faith, with which you can extinguish all the flaming arrows of the evil one. Take the helmet of salvation and the sword of the Spirit, which is the Word of God. And pray in the Spirit on all occasions with all kinds of prayers and requests. With this in mind, be alert and always keep on praying for all the saints" (Ephesians 6:10-18).

We are commanded by the King to arise with our ammunition designed purposely for this combat and to win, for His favor in upon us.

- **The Helmet of Salvation** – A casing over our minds, our thought life.

This is where the battle is taking place every moment of your life. We have been saved, sanctified, forgiven and declared righteous. However, we are in a constant battle with the enemy. Never allow the enemy to tell you are not worthy. It is by His grace that we are what we are today. Protect your mind. Always cover it with the Blood of the Lamb. Remove all the mediocre mindsets you came to Christ with, and allow Him to rule over your mind. (Romans 12:1, 2)

- **The Breast-Plate of Righteousness** – A protection over our hearts

The heart is the seat of our affections. Guard your heart with all diligence. It is the seat of your life. Let the peace of Christ rule your heart and mind. Do not allow the enemy to sow any root of bitterness or of unrighteousness in your heart. Let your heart be His royal throne. (Proverbs 4:23)

- **The Shield of Faith** – A defense on what we stand for.

This is what we stand for. We need to stand for Biblical principles, Biblical virtues and values, and then live by faith. The Bible says:

"Without faith it is impossible to please the Lord, for anyone who comes to the Lord must believe that He exists and that He rewards those who seek Him diligently" (Hebrews 11:6).

Please, never live your life by what you see in the natural. Live through the eyes of God. Act upon what He says, not how you feel or what you see. We must "Contend earnestly for the faith that was once for all entrusted to the saints" (Jude 3), and stand firm on His Word.

- **The Sword of the Spirit** – Our sole authority - The Word of God

We believe that the Word of God is our sole 'authority and rule for faith and conduct.' Nothing less! It stands alone by itself and does not need any defender. We do well to heed its contents and confess our faith in this living and active Word of God.

"For the word of God is living and active. Sharper than any double-edged sword, it penetrates even to dividing soul and spirit, joints and marrow; it judges the thoughts and attitudes of the heart. Nothing in all creation is hidden from God's sight. Everything is uncovered and laid bare before the eyes of Him to whom we must give account" (Hebrews 4:12-13).

"But what does it say? "The Word is near you; it is in your mouth and in your hear," that is, the Word of faith we are proclaiming" (Romans 10:

You can overcome the enemy through the Word. The Master Himself used the Word to defeat the enemy's purpose when he tempted Him in the desert. With the Shield of Faith and the Sword of the Spirit, our hands are filled. We are occupied for the Master's use. There is no place for the enemy in our lives. Our confession and faith in God and His Word, in the finished work of Christ at Calvary, grant us the rights for victory in the name of Jesus, and through the blood (Revelation 12:10).

- **The Belt of Truth** –- Our standard of living – The lifestyle of Christ.

We are encouraged to be truthful to the Lord and to one another. Live in the truth you have received. Walk in the truth, and be truthful to yourself in your walk with the Lord. (Ephesians 4:22-32; 5:1-17 and Colossians 3:1-17).

- **The Gospel Shoes** –- Our walk and our work.

Walking the walk, living the life, and bringing souls into the Kingdom is our reason for being a Christian. We have been commissioned to go into the entire world to preach the gospel, starting from our Jerusalem, which is our home, our families, our neighbors, our co-workers, et cetera. It is a command that should be heeded. We should not be ashamed to preach the Word and to defend the name of Christ. The Name is worth dying for. We are His witnesses. And like Paul, woe unto us if we preach not the gospel (Romans 1:16-18).

We have also been called to live at peace with every body, yet not compromising the Truth. For *'blessed are the peacemakers, for they shall be called the children of God'* (Matthew 5:19). The Bible encourages us to live at peace with everyone and live in holiness, without which no man shall see the Lord (Hebrews 12:14). Living at peace with others despite our differences, is a mark of Christ-likeness (Romans 14:17; John 13:34-35). The world will automatically listen to the gospel when they see Christ being lived out in us.

- **His Presence** – Our welfare and protection.

The Lord did not provide anything for our backs. It is because He Himself is backing us up. Romans 8:31 says, *"If God be for us who can be against us?"* The Lord Himself is behind us, but there is a warning here. Do not turn your back to the enemy and run when the battle becomes strong and fierce. The adversary will hit you on the back. You are not fighting in your own victory. Victory has already been acquired. You are only fighting in His victory, but you need to know who your enemy is, and stand firm to defeat his strategies and purposes.

- **Pray, pray and pray!** – Prayer is our strength and our spiritual breath. (Isaiah 40:31).

You cease breathing when you die. Likewise, if you cease praying you die spiritually. Jesus said in Luke 18:1 *"Men ought always to pray and not to faint."* Before He went to the cross, the last words Jesus told the disciples were,

"Watch and pray, that ye enter not into temptation. The spirit indeed is willing but the flesh is weak" (Matthew 26:41).

Prayer, as said earlier, should be our number one priority task. We need to keep the communication line with the King open 24/24. He Himself promised saying, "Call upon me and I will answer you and show you great and mighty things you do not know" (Jeremiah 33:3). Help is always there. Praise the Lord! We have an advocate before the Father who intercedes for us and represents us before God.

- **The Blood** – The Timed bomb the enemy fears.

The Bible says, "And they overcame him by the blood of the Lamb, and by the word of their testimony." The power in the blood of our Lord is one of the greatest weapons the enemy fears. He trembles at the mention of the blood. His kingdom shakes at the mention of the blood, and his adepts take shelter when confronted with the blood they die sometimes if they become hard-hearted.

In 1979, my husband and I were pastors in a small village in Kame, Togo. We had begun constructing a new edifice for the Lord as a result of the many conversions in Kame and the surrounding villages. One morning, Geoffrey traveled to Lome to purchase building materials for the church. I was left alone with our two sons at that time. About 1.30 in the morning, in the middle of the night, the Lord woke me up to pray. Praying in the Spirit, I submerged the boys first of all in the blood, and continued to intercede.

However, at the same time, I saw a bright fire-like light reflecting on the window. I intensified my prayers. In an instant, I heard someone call my name through the fire by the window. It sent chills into my spine, and goosebumps all over me. Something in me told me not to respond. I continued to pray in the Spirit. I perceived that was the enemy at work. As I pulled myself up to sit on the bed to continue the combat, I heard my name again. This time it was for real. It sounded evil, and demonic. I knew I was into a terrible warfare. At that moment, a holy bold anger swelled up within me. I spoke out. *"The blood of Jesus rebukes you. The blood of Jesus comes against you right now! I send the fire of the Holy Ghost against you. ..."*

Wow! A heard a weird scream! Someone began moaning and saying, "Don't kill me. Please, don't kill me."

I continued to pray; sending the blood and the fire of His presence against the witch behind my window. The fire died down right away, but the moaning persisted for a while. Gradually, everywhere became calm.

"Who is it?" I asked the Lord.

"The town witch," He said. "He came to kill you, but My blood almost killed him. I have given him a chance to repent and to live right. If he does, he will live. However, if he refused to repent, he will die."

I began to praise the Lord. I was literally singing "There is power, power, wonder-working power in the blood" on top of my voice worshipping the Lord at that time of the day. It was about 2.30 a.m. Then the Lord told me that the man would come back the next day to confess Him as Lord, because of the power in His blood.

Geoffrey arrived at about 2.30 in the afternoon. But the news of the man groaning in pain in the village was spreading like wild fire. He had already tried most of the Christians that same night, and could not kill anyone one of them. I narrated the event to Geoffrey and we prayed.

Six o'clock prompt in the night, we heard a knock on our bamboo gate. Geoffrey rushed to check on the stranger behind the gate. There stood Mr. Titi. He'd covered part of his face with a piece of cloth. They exchanged greetings. Geoffrey ushered him inside the compound and gave him a chair. Titi was trembling beyond reasoning.

"What do you want me to do for you?' Geoffrey interrogated.

"I want to give my life to God," he said.

"To God! Why?"

"I don't want to die." He said trembling.

"Why did you decide just in one day to give your life to Jesus?" Geoffrey wanted to get everything out of him. Just the mention of Jesus threw Titi into a shock.

"I, I came to, to take your wife ...." He said stammering through.

Finally after much interrogation, Geoffrey led him to confess his sins and to accept Christ. But what actually threw me overboard was when Geoffrey laid his hand on his head to pray. The witch screamed and wailed in agony saying, "I am burning up! I am burning up!"

Later that day, Amega Titi, and his youngest wife, including some of the children surrendered their lives fully to Christ. His voodoo house was pulled down and burned with fire. This miracle of the power in the blood brought many to the saving knowledge of the Lord Jesus Christ.

Understand that Titi was the head of all the witches in that sub region. When he gave his life to Jesus, the enemy lost a battalion. Today one of his sons is a pastor with the Assemblies of God in Togo. Praise the Lord.

There is power in the blood. It speaks power! It speaks deliverance! It speaks healing! It chases demons away! It speaks the language of the spirit realm. And it is more powerful than any weapon man can ever manufacture, because it works in the physical and in the invisible. It worked in the time of Moses. It worked during the time of the Apostles. It worked in the 1970's and it works even today.

Recently, I woke up in the middle of the night about 1:30 with a terrible chest pain. It radiated through my left arm, and vibrated to my neck. I felt I was having heart attack. The moment I asked myself, "Monica, are you having heart attack?" I believe the enemy heard it, and began speaking to my subconscious. I could hear his demonic voice, "Prepare. You are going to die soon. Call the children and wish them all your best and go to heaven in peace. ... After all you are lonely. ...." It was terrifying.

I was gasping for breath, and felt I was really going to die. I could not think right; so I was about to believe the lie, when I heard the Spirit of God speak to me. "Monica, you will be what you believe. You are what you believe. ..."

Wow! It went through me like a sharp knife. I caught the Rhema Word. It sunk deep into my soul, and struggling to gain momentum, I began whispering, *"The Blood! I plead the blood over my heart, over my body, over my spirit, and over my soul. The blood is still speaking for me. I will not die. I will live to declare the works of the Lord in the land of the living. The blood paid for my health in full. The blood, the blood ...."*

I continued to apply the blood on every organ in my body in the name of Jesus. I knelt by the bed and continued with my proclamations. I stood on my ground even though the pain intensified, and the enemy continued to taunt me. All of a sudden, something broke in the realm of the spirit. His peace began to flood over my soul, and I began to sing. When I looked at the time, it was exactly 4:25 a.m. I climbed the bed and stretched myself in the middle of the bed, my feet hanging at the edge, and went to sleep. I woke up at eight exhausted from the combat, but well and strong. Praise God! I am still standing with the Precious Blood.

- **The Name of The LORD JESUS CHRIST.**

"Therefore God exalted Him to the highest place and gave Him the Name that is above every name, that at the name of Jesus every knee should bow in heaven and on earth and under the earth, and every tongue confess that Jesus Christ is Lord, to the glory of God the Father" (Philippians 1:9-11).

Salvation is found in His name. Through His Name, we gain access to the Father. Through His Name, Heaven's portals flung open. Healing comes through His Name. His Name brings comfort. His Name produces miracles. His Name drives away the enemy. Angels bow at His name. All hell and its demons run into hiding when His Name is mentioned. Peace comes, when we call upon that wonderful Name. Fight through His name. There is no demon that can defeat you when He shows up.

We have a small chorus in Africa, which sends a serious message to the camp of the enemy when we begin to sing it.

> That Wonderful Name, Jesus
> That Wonderful Name, Jesus
> That Wonderful Name, Jesus
> There is no other Name I know

Sister, take the Name of Jesus with you everywhere, anywhere, and at all times. Jesus is our Shelter in the time of the storm. Jesus is our Hiding Place. Jesus is our Strong Tower. We find refuge in Him.

"He who dwells in the shadow in the shelter of the Most High will rest in the shadow of the Almighty. I will say of the Lord, "He is my refuge and my fortress, my God in whom I trust. Surely He will save you from the fowler's snare and from the deadly pestilence. He will cover you with His feathers, and under His wings you will find refuge; His faithfulness will be your shield and rampart. You will not fear the terror of night, nor the arrow that flies by day, nor the pestilence that stalks in the darkness, nor the plague that destroys at midday. A thousand may fall at your side, ten thousand at your right hand, but it will not come near you. You will only observe with your eyes and see the punishment of the wicked

... "Because **he loves me,**" says the Lord, "**I will rescue him; I will protect him, for he acknowledges My name. He will call upon Me, and I will answer him; I will be with him in trouble, I will deliver him and honor him.** With long life will I satisfy him and show him My salvation.'"(Psalms 91 summarized – emphasis mine).

When He is in the boat, life's storm will never ever be able to drown us. Say the Name and mean it and you will never regret calling out to Him. Many books have been written about the Name. It will help if you can get a copy. The demons in the man in the book of Acts knew who Jesus was (Acts 19:14-16). The possessed man in the Gerasenes knew who Jesus was (Matthew 8:28-34). And they know Him even today (Mark 5:1-20; James 2:19).

- **Praise – A Mighty Weapon of War, of Triumph, and Victory.**

"Praise ye the Lord. Sing unto the Lord a new song, and His praise in the congregation of saints... Let the saints be joyful in glory: let them sing aloud upon their beds. Let the praises of God be in their mouths, and a two-edged sword in their hand; to execute vengeance upon the heathen, and punishments upon the people; to bind their kings with chains, and their nobles with fetters of iron; to execute upon them judgment written: this honour have all His saints. Praise ye the Lord" (Psalms 149:1, 5-9).

To praise God means, to preoccupy with Who God is, what He has done, and what He can do for His glory. To praise God, is to express admiration, gratitude, and adoration to His Majesty, the Creator of heaven and earth for His surpassing greatness. To praise the Lord, is to thank Him for answered prayers, and to worship Him for what we expect Him to do for us. In whatever way, praises gladden the heart of God.

God is always with us according to Matthew 28:20. However, praises actually allow the presence of God to manifest in a greater dimension. Praises bring God down to act, to fight, and to bring victory to His children. King David wrote, "Seven times a day do I praise Thee because of Thy righteous judgments" (Psalms 119:164).

Why should we praise the Lord? "I don't feel like it sometimes," you may say. In spite of how we feel, we need to praise the Lord because,

- God deserves our praises. He is worthy of all our praises (Psalms 48:1).
- He is our Maker, our God, and we are His people. He is the King of all kings, and reigns above all of His creation (Psalms 95:1-7).
- God is enthroned in our praise. Psalms 22:3 says, "But Thou art holy, O Thou that inhabitest the praises of Israel."
- God is good and merciful. It is by His grace and mercy that we are still alive (Psalms 100; Psalms 103:1-5; Psalms 107).
- We were created for God's praise and pleasure (Revelations 4:11; Jeremiah 13:11; 1 Peter 2:9). When we praise the Lord, we express our love, our acceptance of His Supremacy and Lordship over us.
- Praise is a command. If you are breathing, it is a must for you to praise the Lord. Psalms 150 verse 6 says, "Let everything that has breath praise the Lord."
- Praise opens the door for more of God's blessings in our lives (Deuteronomy 8:10-18).

- Praise is a healthy recommendation for saints (Psalms 92:1-5). It ignites healing and miracles in our personal and emotional lives.
- Dead bodies cannot praise the Lord (Psalms 115:17).
- Praise is our sacrifices to God. However, if we refuse to praise God, God is capable of raising up stones to lift up His name (Jeremiah 17:26; Jeremiah 33:3-11).
- Praise is a mighty weapon of prayer (1 Chronicles 5:13-14; 2 Chronicles 20:15-29; Acts 16:25-28). Praise brings deliverance. Praise brings blessings and victory. Praise brings miracles!

There were many instances in the Bible, where God literally descended in His glory, and brought complete victory to His people through praises and worship. In 2 Chronicles 5:13-14, the glory of God came down literally as His people praised Him with all kinds of instruments. God's glory filled the temple because His people entered His presence with His heart's desires—praise and adoration. We read,

> "It came to pass, as the trumpeters and singers were as one, to make one sound to be heard in praising and thanking the LORD; and when they lifted up their voices with the trumpets and cymbals and instrument of music, and praised the LORD, saying, 'For He is good; and His mercy endureth for ever:' that then the house was filled with a cloud; even the house of the LORD; so that the priests could not stand to minister by reason of the cloud; for the glory of the LORD had filled the house of God."

In the case of king Jehoshaphat, Judah's three great enemies—the Moabites, the Ammonites, and the Edomites, surrounded Judah to annihilate them. They came in such great multitude, king Jehoshaphat feared greatly. Actually, his fears drew him and the people to seek the face of the Lord in prayer and fasting (2 Chronicles 20:1-13). In the midst of their prayers and supplication, God sent a word through the prophet Jahaziel.

"...Hearken ye, all Judah, and ye inhabitants of Jerusalem, and thou king Jehoshaphat, 'Thus saith the Lord unto you, be not afraid nor dismayed by reason of this great multitude; for the battle is not yours, but God's. Ye shall not need to fight in this battle: set yourselves, stand ye still, and see the salvation of the Lord with you, O Judah and Jerusalem; tomorrow go out against them; for the LORD will be with you'" (2 Chronicles 20:15-17).

Jehoshaphat believed the word of the Lord given, and bowed his head to the ground; and all Judah also joined him to worship the Lord. He then charged the people to believe in the Lord their God, and in His prophets. Finally, he appointed singers to sing and praise the Lord before the army as they match to battle.

I believe this procedure was in the package of deliverance. And so the moment they began to sing and praise Him, the Lord set ambushment against their enemies, and they were smitten before them. The children of Ammon and Moab became so confused that they began to destroy the Edomites; then they turned around to destroy one another (2 Chronicles 20:22-25). God literally sent down angelic hosts to discomfit the enemies to their own destruction, because God inhabits in the praises of His people.

The next time God came down and brought great deliverance to His servants, was in a Philippian jail. In the book of Acts chapter 16, Paul and Silas were preaching the Word of God in the city of Philippi. There arose a problem. Satan stirred up an agent who followed them daily declaring, "These are the servants of the Most High, which show us the way of salvation" (Acts 16:7). Her predictions in a sense, was accurate, because Paul and Silas were truly God's servant.

However, this act of the damsel was to discredit the message of the gospel, by making the people think they were in league with demonic spirit, which was at work in the girl and were healing the sick through the devil. You see, it was believed (and still is), that all who pretended to tell the future were influenced by a god or a spirit. Fortune telling is not of God, and God hates it (Deuteronomy 18:9-14).

Paul took action in the power of His name. The girl was set free, but not her masters. Her masters caused great commotion. Paul and Silas were beaten and thrown into prison. At midnight, Paul and Silas began to pray, and to sing praises to God. Praise the Lord! He showed up with an earthquake. Let's read this interesting breakthrough through prayer and praises.

> "And at midnight Paul and Silas prayed, and sang praises to God: and the prisoners heard them. And suddenly there was a great earthquake, so that the foundations of the prison were shaken; and immediately all the doors were opened, and everyone's bands were loosed" (Acts 16:25-26).

God answered their prayers. He intervened through their praises by sending a great earthquake, opening all the prison doors, loosed the bonds of all prisoners, and saved the jailer and his household.

Praises work! Let your Heavenly Daddy hear your voice today. He is awesome and beyond your ability to comprehend His greatness.

QUOTABLE QUOTES

"God is an infinite circle whose center is everywhere and whose circumference is nowhere."

    Saint Augustine of Hippo (354-430)

[14]

ORDINARY, YET EXTRAORDINARY

(Chosen By Grace And For A Purpose!)

❖

"Where is the wise man? Where is the scholar? Where is the philosopher of this age? Has not God made foolish the wisdom of this world? For since in the wisdom of God the world through its wisdom did not know Him, God was pleased through the foolishness of what was preached to save those who believe. ... but to those whom God has called, both Jews and Greeks, Christ the power of God and the wisdom of God. For the foolishness of God is wiser than man's wisdom, and the weakness of God is stronger than man's strength" (I Corinthian 1:20- 25 summarized).

In February 2002, the Lord gave me a vision of a woman holding a globe, having footprints of women and children and young people; and her tears dripping on it. The sky flew open. There was a face inside the cloud looking down weeping. And as the tears dripped on the globe it became like drops of blood. He showed me the pains and heartaches women are going through. He made me to understand that even though women were given His heart for mankind, and women were His instruments of continuing procreation — birthing new lives into the world; physically and spiritually, many are no longer in that position. Many women may never see the fulfillment of their destiny because of the lies the enemy has sown in their hearts.

At that moment, He said to me, "Monica, there is warfare going on right now in the heavens – forces of evil breaking, distracting and diverting My original heart of passion and compassion from women and the younger generation they are supposed to mentor. As a result, many women are broken, feeling rejected, disgraced, discouraged and disappointed. Many hearts are bleeding, but I want them to know that I am doing a new thing with women in these last days. I am restoring all things for My glory. …. "

"…. Restore to her all that was hers and all the fruits of the field, since the day that she left the land, even until now" (II Kings 8:6b KJV).

Apparently, there were four main problems women faced in the past and are still facing today. The first problem is an identity crisis: Who we think we are, or want to be. We struggle with issues of race and color, education or social status, weight and height, and anything one can think of. Because of the struggle to be something else other than what our Creator made us to be, many women have become vulnerable to deception and lies.

Was it not the same problem the first woman faced? Undoubtedly yes! When the devil proposed another way of being something else, greater and better than what God intended for her to be, she fell victim, and pulled Adam into the net. Satan said, "You will be like God." And as a result of the lie the enemy proposed to her, the whole world went under a curse.

However, God wants you to know this, O daughter of the Most High God. Your identity is not in what others think you ought to be. Your identity is not in what you think you want to be, or what you are today. Your identity is not in what society is portraying, advertising, or proposing to you. Your identity is found in what God says you are in Christ Jesus.

Christ Jesus died to connect us back to what we lost in Adam, and to fuse us into God's original plan of being royalties—reigning and seated with Christ in the heavenly places. You are a princess, cherished by God. It doesn't matter which pedigree you may come from. You are a full blooded child of the living God, whether you are black or white, a Jew or a Gentile, tall or short, overweight or slim—whatever, you are very precious to your heavenly Daddy, the King.

The second problem many women struggle with is the feeling of unworthiness. Apparently, this has become another deadly weapon the enemy is using to discourage many women from being what they were created to be. He beats them up everyday with their past failures and mistakes— hence rendering them weak and inefficient in ministry. *"You are not worthy, because of this and that….. You do not have a good testimony at all. ….. Everyone knows who you are and what you've done ….. You do not have any degree. You are not even educated …."*

However, look up. God made you to be a beacon, a guiding light, an inspiration to others around you. You may not be worthy in the sight of men, but you are worthy and important to God because of the blood. Once Christ lives in you, you are no longer under any other condemnation because His word says,

> "There is therefore now no condemnation to them which are in Christ Jesus, who walk not after the flesh, but after the Spirit. For the law of the Spirit of life in Christ Jesus hath made me free from the law of sin death" (Romans 8:1-2).

The third problem, which is the enemy's secret weapon against women, is what "The church" has fashioned many to be. The statement of the apostle Paul, "Let the women be in silence," has been mistakenly translated in such a manner as to keep women out of ministry in some denominational circles. But it is the same apostle, who wrote, *"There is neither Jew nor Greek, there is neither bond nor free, there is neither male nor female: for ye are all one in Christ" (Galatians 3:28)*. Paul labored together with women such as: Phoebe and Priscilla, Lydia and Euódias, and many others.

> "I commend to you our sister **Phoebe**, a servant of the church in Cenchrea. I ask you to receive her in the Lord in a way worthy of the saints and to give her any help she may need from you, for she has been a great help to many people, including me. Greet **Priscilla** and Aquila, my fellow workers in Christ. They risked their lives for me. Not only I but all the churches of the Gentiles are grateful to them. Greet **Mary,** who worked hard for you. Greet **Tryphena** and **Tryphosa**, those women who work hard in the Lord. Greet my dear friend **Persis**, another woman who has worked hard in the Lord. Greet Rufus, ... and **his mother,** who has been a mother to me, too" (Romans 16:1-4, 6, 12-13 emphasis mine).

"I beseech **Euódias,** and beseech **Syntyche,** that they be of the same mind in the Lord. ...help those women which labored with me in the gospel, ..." (Philippians 4:2-3 emphasis mine).

The last deadly weapon is the negative cultural influence of modern society. Could you believe that in today's world of sophisticated technology and civilization, women are treated like "things" as opposed to humans in some cultural circles? A careful look at many women in non democratic nations, gives us a glimpse of their many sufferings in other lands.

There have been cultural and religious prejudices that have hindered the call of God as it pertains to women in the past. Throughout history women were classified as being back bench sitters, baby makers, house keepers, et cetera. These mighty walls of human ideologies and religious sexism, erected against women, is being crumbled by the Holy Spirit, because God is raising up for Himself a mighty army of women from all around the world. They are living brands plugged out of the fires. Though they carry on their hearts and spirit deep wounds, and scars, bruises, and ashes of their past, they have now been refined and they carry His heart to impact this generation for Christ. They are God's axe heads, who are ready to snatch this generation from the hands of the enemy. They have deep intimacy with the King of kings. They are women, who know that the only way to have authority in the spirit realm, to overcome satan, and to command obedience in this physical world, is to live under authority. Yes, they have come to understand that to have authority means to possess the legal rights to enforce obedience effectively in others as written in 2 Corinthians 10:4-6. When obedience to God and man is complete, any woman can be effective in her calling.

As said earlier, God used a Gentile woman, Ruth to become the breaker of the wall of separation (erected to hinder God's pre-ordained purposes for humanity), thereby pre-fulfilling Apostle Paul's revelation of no distinction in Christ. Paul wrote, *"For ye are all the children of God by faith in Christ Jesus. ... There is neither Jew nor Greek, there is neither bond nor free, there is neither male nor female: for ye are all one in Christ. And if ye be Christ's, then are ye Abraham's seed, and heirs according to the promise"* (Galatians 3:26-29 summarized)

Charles Colson said, "When the church fails to break the [cultural] barrier, both sides loses. Those who need the gospel message of hope and the reality of love, don't get it, and the isolated church keeps evangelizing the same people over and over until its only mission finally is to entertain itself... When the church transcends culture, it can transform culture."

THE ORDINARY, EXTRAORDINARY VESSEL

"Before I formed you in the womb I knew you, before you were born I set you apart; I appointed you as a prophet to the nations."

"Do not say, 'I am only a child.' You must go to everyone I send you to and say whatever I command you. Do not be afraid of them, for I am with you and will rescue you," declares the Lord. Then the Lord reached out His hand and touched my mouth and said to me, 'Now, I have put My words in your mouth. See, today I appoint you over nations and kingdoms to uproot and tear down, to destroy and overthrow, to build and to plant. Get yourself ready! Stand up and say to them whatever I command you. Do not be terrified by them, or I will terrify you before them. Today, I have made you a fortified city, an iron pillar and a bronze wall to stand against the whole land .... They will fight against you but will not overcome you, for I am with you and will rescue you'" (Jeremiah 1:5-19 summarized).

There is a mighty army of women rising in the horizon. There is a forceful spiritual army of women who are rising up with the heart of God for this generation. But who are they? What about the coming army which is rising up?

This mighty army of women the Lord is gathering for Himself from around the world are mighty giants, although men may not recognize their worth. They are ordinary women, yet they are extraordinary in the sight of the Father, our King. It is not hard to find them. They are everywhere around the world. They are 'common' house wives. They are house cleaners. They are store clerks, and restaurant servers. Some are toilets cleaners, and trash collectors. They may be low-classes or low-born. Others are professionals, entrepreneurs, Presidents, Secretary of States, ambassadors, et cetera. None of these matters to God.

These women have one thing in common. They know the God of the Bible, and they have made themselves available to be used in one way or other. They know it. Deep down in their hearts they know they have a mission to accomplish.

The revival which occurred on Azuza streets, sheds light on what the Holy Spirit is about to do before the coming of the Lord. Many women were instrumental in the birth of this revival. They were prayer warriors, who were filled with the Holy Spirit. They preached all around this nation, proclaiming the Lordship of Christ and His coming Kingdom. They were so full of the anointing and zeal that nothing could stop them from the proclamation of the Truth, the Way and the Life they had known. They had absolute authority and power over the works of the devil and represented God among men. All their desires were absorbed in one thing: God's glory. And this the army God is raising up for His glory.

Remember, The King's end-time daughters are "Spiritual Hijackers!" They do not destroy the lives of others, but with their spiritual ammunition, they are always armed, ready for action to take back what the enemy has stolen from God's children, and to bring others into the kingdom of God. They are armed!

"Then the Lord reached out His hand and touched my mouth and said to me, "Now I have put My words in your mouth. See today I appoint you over nations and kingdoms to uproot and tear down, to destroy and overthrow, to build and to plant. ... Get yourself ready! Stand up and say to them whatever I command you. Do not be terrified by them, or I will terrify you before them. ..." (Jeremiah 1:9-10, 17)

They are ready to defy the enemy like Jael — Not with force but by diplomacy and the demonstration of the power of God. Jael used courtesy to crush the head of the enemy of her people (Judges 4:17-24). They are ready to snatch their children from the clutches of the enemy like the Syrophoenician woman who came to Jesus. They never give up until they see the result (Mark 7:25-31).

They are ready to fast, pray, and act like Esther until they see victory. (Please, read the book of Esther and see how God used her to save her people). They are ready to forsake all things like Ruth in order to be a blessing to someone else. They are ready to be willing vessels that will only sow peace instead of strife like Abigail (I Samuel 25).

They are ready to stir up revival everywhere they go, because their bones are even filled with the anointing like Elisha (2 Kings 13:20-21). They are ready to be living sacrifices like Jephthah's daughter (Judges 11:29-40). They are ready to pass on the mantles of leadership to this younger generation. They are mentors, like Timothy's mother and grandmother, Eunice and Lois (II Timothy 1:5).

So before we conclude, let's take a last glance at some of these Biblical extraordinary women. What do you think these women of God we read about in the Bible were?

Who in reality was Ruth? She was a forerunner — representing the Church. She was redeemed by Boaz who became her husband and foreshadowed the redemptive work of Christ. Her marriage to Boaz spiritually and prophetically depicts the merging of Gentiles and Jew to form the Body of Christ.

Who actually was Esther? She was a time changer. Had Esther been selfish, Israel would have been annihilated by Haman and their enemies. She did not count her life precious when it became necessary for her to do the impossible to save her people. She made history and changed the time of her day for God's glory.

Who really was Miriam? She was a presence-carrier. She served as a prophetess. Her intimacy with God made Miriam a worshipper, who led the people of Israel in praise to the Almighty after the crossing of the Red sea.

Who in point of fact was Anna? She was a Spiritual firefighter. She did not allow her pain to keep her from the presence of the Lord. She fought through intercession till she saw the birth of the Messiah.

Who in fact was Deborah? She was a mighty combatant—a warrior. She was a judge, a mother in Israel, and an inspirer, whose ministry pushed men and women to the fore-front to defeat Israel's enemies.

Who was Mary, the mother of Christ? She was The Word carrier. Mary, clothed with humility accepted the difficult task to carry The Word becoming flesh, and to birth the God-Son. Knowing the consequence of being stoned for being unfaithful and inevitable ridicule from her people even if

Joseph accepted her as wife, she stood on the Word given by the Angel, and brought forth EMMANUEL — God with us.

Who was this Dorcas? She was an ordinary giver—God's hand extended; supporting the poor and the widows, yet her ministry of clothing the poor, caught God's attention. She was brought back to life because she was remembered for impacting other lives.

Who are you? You are an ordinary person, born of God, filled with His Spirit, and called to impact lives!

Clarence. W. Hatch wrote, "There are many who profess to love God and his cause but are not dedicated to it. They go to church regularly. They read their Bibles. They pray that the work of the Lord will be carried to all corners of the earth. They give tithes and offerings on occasion. They participate in the church services and call themselves Christian, but are they actually willing to share, to give their best for Christ's cause? On every hand there is need for an understanding of all-out consecration of the faculties God has given us. Without this consecration, God cannot work in us and through us to accomplish his purpose in our lives or in the world."

Whatever God has called you to do is very important to the Father. Is it to be an intercessor? Do it for the Father. Is it to be an encourager? Put all your effort into it for Christ sake. Whatever your hands find to do, do it with all your might for the King is coming soon (Ecclesiastes 9:10).

This call is a call to an unlimited service in the Father's house, and to the world. It is a call, which covers every aspect of our efforts for the cause of the Kingdom. There are no restraints or restrictions; no educational qualifications and titles; all He wants is our availability. Whoever you are, please, wake up to the dawn. He used fishermen. He used tax-collectors. He used lawyers. He used housewives. He used slave girls; and He is still looking out for people like us to advance His Kingdom. Charles Wesley composed,

A charge to keep I have
A God to glorify
A never dying soul to save
And fit it for the sky

To serve the present age
My calling to fulfill
O may it all my powers engage
To do my Master's will

Help me to watch and pray
As in Thyself rely
Assured if I my trust betrayed
I shall forever die

QUOTABLE QUOTES

"God entrusted His reputation to ordinary people. Yet in some way invisible to us, these ordinary people filled with the Spirit are helping to restore the universe to its place under the reign of God. ..."

Philip Yancey (1949-)

[15]

THE FINAL WORD

(Acquire Wisdom, Knowledge and Understanding)

❖

"Blessed is the man who finds wisdom, the man who gains understanding, for she is more profitable than silver and yields better returns than gold. She is more precious than rubies; nothing you desire can compare with her. Long life is in her right hand; in her left hand are riches and honor. ... She is a tree of life to those who embrace her; those who lay hold of her will be blessed" (Proverbs 3:13-18).

"He has showed you, O man, what is good. And what does the Lord require of you? To act justly and to love mercy and to walk humbly with your God" (Micah 6:8).

It is said that, "Knowledge is power." Yet, knowledge without a deep revelation of Who God is, and what He requires from His children, leads to foolishness, selfishness, and self-centeredness. Knowledge without discernment and discretion as to how one should deal with fellow human beings, leads to pride and arrogance, and all evil works.

Many high ranked individuals ended their lives prematurely, because, although they had worldly knowledge, they lacked a deeper understanding of what they were created to be. They were ranked "Intellectuals" yet they lacked the fear of God and reverence for the Word of God. They were deficient of discernment, as they treated fellow human beings, created in the image of God, as "animals and slaves." They became prideful to think of themselves as being superior to others. In their arrogance, they declared that "There is no God." They took the place of God and made of themselves 'god,' and became futile in their own thoughts, thus ending their lives, or that of others in pain and misery.

"Knowledge is power" in the sense, that it gives one access to the highest positions in life. On the other hand, remember that knowledge of the Lord gives every believer greater power and unlimited access into the realm of the invisible, to overcome any obstacle in life. True knowledge of God gives the believer the ability to love God, and love others without discrimination, and God gives him or her free access to everything that is His. God then defines who you are, and what He can use you to become for His glory.

True wisdom, true knowledge, and true understanding of His Majesty, and one's purpose on earth, will actually ignite a deep desire to live a meaningful life, led by the Spirit of God. So in acquiring wisdom, knowledge, and understanding, please, walk always in the influence of the Spirit of God. His Spirit will enable you to produce the desired fruit that will bless the heart of God, and that of others. For "The fruit of the Spirit is, *love, joy, peace, longsuffering, gentle-*

ness, goodness, faith, meekness, temperance: against such there is no law" (Galatians 5:22-23).

To dissect the real meaning of this fruit of the Spirit, let's see what a Bible *commentator has to say.

- **Love**: Gr. agape – divine love. A strong, ardent, tender, compassionate, devotion to the well being of someone (I Corinthians 13:4).
- **Joy**: Gr. chara – the emotional excitement, gladness, delight over blessings received or expected for self and for others (Luke 1:41-56).
- **Peace**: Gr. eirene – the state of quietness, rest, repose, harmony, order, and security in the midst of turmoil, strife, and temptations (Isaiah 26:3; John 14:27).
- **Longsuffering**: Gr. makrothumia - patient endurance; to bear long the frailties, offences, injuries, and provocations of others, without murmuring, repining, or resentment (1 Corinthians 13:4-7; 1Timothy 1:16; 2 Timothy 3:10-13; 1 Peter 1:6-7).
- **Gentleness**: Gr. chrestotes – a disposition to be gentle, soft-spoken, kind, even-tempered, cultured, and refined in character and conduct (2 Timothy 2:24-2; Titus 3:1-4).
- **Goodness**: Gr. agathosune – the state of being good, kind, virtuous, benevolent, generous, and God-like in life and conduct (Matthew 5:43-48; Ephesians 5:8-10).
- **Faith**: Gr. pistis – the living, divinely implanted, acquired, and created principle of inward and wholehearted confidence, assurance, trust, and reliance in God, and all that He says (Hebrews 11:1-6).
- **Meekness**: Gr. praotes – the disposition to be gentle, kind, indulgent, even balanced in tempers and passions, and patient in suffering injuries without

feeling a spirit of revenge (Psalms 25:9; Matthew 5:5).
- **Temperance:** Gr.enkrateia – self control; a moderation in the indulgence of the appetites and passions (1Corinthians 9:25-27; Philippians 4:5). *(Taken from The Dake Annotated Reference Bible pg 206 – King James Version)

Someone wrote, "Saints are those who flow in the Spirit of God."

"Knowledge is power" when Christ becomes the wisdom of God to you. So get knowledge (have a clear perception of who God is), get wisdom (using good judgment), and understanding (to comprehend what the will of God is). Acquire a deep knowledge of Who God is, and live your life each day with deep reverence for God, and deep love for fellow human beings.

In the dictionary, "Wisdom" is defined as "Using good judgment, and knowing what is true."

"Knowledge" (n) is "the result or condition of knowing; clear perception; learning, information, skill, acquaintance." "To know" (vt) means to perceive with certainty, to understand; to be aware of; to distinguish; to be acquainted with; to have experience of; To have knowledge; and not doubtful.

"Understand" (vt) To comprehend, to see through; to suppose to mean, to infer; to recognize as implied although not expressed, —vi. to comprehend, learn.

So in the simple definition of these three words, we can only say with the sage Solomon, "Wisdom is the principal thing, therefore get wisdom: and with all thy getting get understanding. Exalt her and she shall promote thee: she shall bring thee honor, when thou dost embrace her. She shall give to thine head an ornament of grace: a crown of glory shall she deliver to thee" (Proverbs 4:7-9).

The Bible declares, "By Wisdom the Lord laid the earth's foundation, by Understanding He set the heavens in place; by His Knowledge the deeps were divided, and the clouds let drop the dew. My son, do not let wisdom and understanding out of your sight, preserve sound judgment and discretion; they will be life for you, an ornament to grace your neck. Then you will go on your way in safety, and your foot will not stumble" (Proverbs 3:19-21).

Acquiring true wisdom, true knowledge, and real understanding in the fear of God, is an unending treasure every woman needs to follow after. They will preserve us from spiritual and moral disaster.

"Let us hear the conclusion of the whole matter: Fear God, and keep His commandments: for this is the whole duty of man. For God shall bring every work into judgment, with every secret thing, whether it be good, or whether it be evil" (Ecclesiastes 12:13-14).

Paul Tournier (1898-1986) wrote, *"We do not have to give up our reason, our intelligence, our knowledge, our faculty to judge, nor our emotions, our likes, our desires, our instincts, our conscious and unconscious aspirations, but rather to place them all in God's hands, so that He may direct, stimulates, fertilize, develop, and use them."*

* * * * * * *

Finally, sisters, the expected anointing upon women will not displace the authority and protection of your husbands upon you if you are married. Neither will it make you superior to your pastor and spiritual leaders. For without any authority over your life, you will make yourself vulnerable to the attack of the enemy as you remove yourself from God's protection. It is true that in Christ there is no male or female, free or bond, however, God holds all of us accountable in regard to hierarchy.

> "Submit to one another out of reverence for Christ. Wives, submit to your husbands as to the Lord. For the husband is the head of the wife as Christ is the head of the church, His body, of which He is the Savior. Now as the church submits to the Christ, so also wives should submit to their husbands in everything" (Ephesians 5:21-24).

Authority is God's idea and not mine. You can verify this information from Prophetess Miriam and her brother Aaron in Numbers 12:1-16. I believe the greater the anointing, the humbler one should become.

These end-time daughters of the King are not liberated from their God-given responsibility of being submissive to their own husbands and of being God-fearing mothers. Rather through the anointing they will impact their families, their communities, and their nations to the glory and honor of our Lord and Savior Jesus Christ.

TO BE CONTINUED

Now, to be continued .... Why? This book is not an end in itself. It is only a message delivered to the daughters of the King. The Holy Spirit is still writing His book on human heart, commissioning and awakening His church for an end-time revival till Christ appears in the sky for His church. Jean-Pierre de Caussade wrote,

> "The books the Holy Spirit is writing are living, and every soul a volume in which the divine author makes a true revelation of His word, explaining it to every heart, unfolding it in every moment."

To be continued ……….. Why? Christ is coming for a glorious Church without spot or wrinkle. He is calling out a people who are selfless and spotless, and who are willing to pay the price no matter what.

To be continued ………. Why? Because the book of Acts is still being written by those who have chosen to live by the Spirit—in obeying the voice of the One who is calling out a people, who are ready to turn the world right side up for His glory.

To be continued ……… Why? Because this is harvest time! Go forth in His name. "And they went forth, and preached everywhere, the Lord working with them and confirming the word with signs following. A-men" (Mark 16:20).

"He who has an ear, let Him hear what the Spirit is saying to His church."

CAN THIS BE YOUR DAILY PROCLAMATION?

I am the daughter of the King. I am highly favored. I am deeply cherished by God. I am blessed beyond all my past circumstances and failures. I have a higher calling, and I will fulfill my destiny through Christ Jesus my Lord. I declare that I am victorious! I have triumphantly overcome the enemy, the flesh and all obstacles in life through Christ Jesus. I will never be defeated! I am walking on my high places. I am blessed today. Tomorrow I will be blessed. My future is blessed. Whatever my hands touch for Christ will be blessed. I am blessed to be a blessing in Christ Name. I am being restored seven fold of all that the enemy stole from me according to His Word. I know no defeat! I am His hands extended, and His heart expressed to a lost and dying world, and I will be His instrument of righteousness as long as I live. In

Christ Name I make this declaration, and so be it. Amen.

MARANATHA, JESUS IS COMING SOON! May He alone be exalted in our lives as we wait for His glorious appearing! Amen.

THE WORD OF THE LORD

"Behold, I am coming soon! My reward is with Me, and I will give to everyone according to what he has done. I am the Alpha and the Omega, the First and the Last, the Beginning and the End. Blessed are those who wash their robes, that they may have the right to the tree of life and may go through the gates into the city. Outside are the dogs, those who practice magic arts, the sexually immoral, the murderers, the idolaters and everyone who loves and practices falsehood. ... He who testifies to these things says, "Yes, I am coming soon." Amen. Come, Lord Jesus. The grace of the Lord Jesus be with God's people. Amen" (Revelations 22:12-15, 20-21).

APPENDIX 1

MY REFLECTION

❖

Every child of God knows the story of Ruth and Naomi. But this day, the Holy Spirit gave me new insight about this Gentile woman, Ruth, whose story has been read worldwide, and through her the whole world has been blessed.

It was just a normal day for me. After my usual morning prayer time that normally starts between 2 a.m. and 5 a.m., I felt a strong urge to leave the room in order to study my Bible. I had already started reading through the whole Bible starting from Genesis to the Book of Judges, and I found out that my next book was Ruth. I wanted to skip it when I heard the Lord speak to my heart saying: *"Monica, how much do you know about Ruth that you want to skip? Open it wide and I will show you what I am asking from My daughters of this end-time."*

Prayerfully, I began my journey with the Lord through the book of Ruth. He began showing me these Biblical truths I am sharing with all the daughters of God, who want to be part of this end-time revival.

God gives revelations for a purpose. He reveals His plans and purposes, and speaks to His people so they would take the message and run with it. Many are discouraged and downhearted. Souls are dying. We need to rise up from the ashes of our past with this good news of restoration to embrace what He has for us before it is too late.

God has got an army
Matching through the land
Deliverance is their song
With Healing in their hands
Everlasting Joy
Gladness in their hearts
In this army I've got a part!

(From Morris Cerullo's School of Ministry)

God bless you as you face all the challenges to be a mighty warrior of Christ. Amen.

APPENDIX 2

MY LITTLE EXPERIENCE

One of the first words people think of in the American society when they refer to mother-in-law is "difficult". On the contrary, in my experience, when I think of my Mama Monica, the first word that comes to mind is "Love". She has shown me what true love is, even to those who do her wrong. I've seen her sitting in her room with the door shut hours at a time, singing her heart out; worshiping and praying to her Daddy in Heaven. She is an awesome testimony as a wife, a widow, a mother, a pastor, and a mighty woman of God.

Looking at her children, and especially my husband, I know God is, and has been present in her entire inspirational life, raising mighty men and warriors in the Kingdom of God. I am honored to call her Mother-in-law, Mama, and Grandmother to my child. I only pray that by God's grace, I would be compelled to follow after her. She has impacted many women in many nations, and I have been touched by her wisdom, authority, grace, and the love she has so amiably imparted to me. I know this book will impact your life, and you will never be the same. God has anointed her to spread the word to the nations and by His grace, she will.

By Julia (Randolph) Tomtania

QUOTABLE QUOTES

"Lord, make me an instrument of your peace. Where there is hatred, let me sow love; where there is injury, pardon; where there is doubt, faith; where there is despair, hope; where there is darkness, light; and where there is sadness, joy. O divine Master, grant that I may not so much seek to be consoled as to console; to be understood as to understand; to be loved as to love. For it is in giving that we receive; it is in pardoning that we are pardoned and it is in dying that we are born to eternal life."

Saint Francis of Assisi (1181-1226)

BIBLIOGRAPHY/ ACKNOWLEDGEMENT

❖

- ❖ Charles Spurgeon, pg xvii
- ❖ James Russell Miller, pg 37
- ❖ Henry Jowett, pg 51
- ❖ Dr. Samuel D. Gordon, pg 59 From Quiet Talks on Service
- ❖ Joseph Parker, pg 82
- ❖ Charles Stanley, pg 99 – From A Touch of His Wisdom, © 1992, Zondervan Publishing House
- ❖ Bishop Handley Carr Moule, pg 104 & pg 124
- ❖ Sergio Scataglini, pg 109 – From The Fire of His Holiness, Destiny Image Publishers
- ❖ Catherine Jackson, pg 121 – From The Christian's Secret of a Happy Life, © 1979
- ❖ Charles Swindoll, pg 123 – From Draper's Book of Quotations from the Christian World, Edited by Edythe Draper, © 1992, Tyndale House Publishers Inc
- ❖ Teresa of Avila, pg 142
- ❖ Ray Stedman, pg 143 & pg 149 – From Adventures Through The Bible

- ❖ A. W. Tozer, pg 151 & pg 222 – From How To Be Filled With the Holy Spirit & That Incredible Christian, Christian Publication, Camp Hill, Pennsylvania
- ❖ Abraham Lincoln, pg 172
- ❖ Jean Eudes, pg 208
- ❖ William Barclay, pg 243 – From Draper's Book of Quotations from the Christian World © 1992
- ❖ Saint Augustine of Hippo, pg 270
- ❖ Clarence W. Hatch, pg 281 – From Stewardship Enriches Life, © 1951
- ❖ Philip Yancey (1949-) pg 283
- ❖ Paul Tournier (1898-1986) pg 290
- ❖ Saint Francis of Assissi (1181-1226) pg 298

My love for books led me to collect different quotes from various men and women of God - some of which I got from labels, teabags, guidepost and divers works. They've been such an inspiration to me and so I thought of inserting few in this book. Please, where further acknowledgement is needed, I will make any adjustment to insert it in a future publication. Thanks and may the Lord bless you richly for being such an instrument of blessing.

Printed in the United States
201560BV00002B/1-99/P